TO HELIGOLAND AND BEYOND!

Punk Rock Tour Diaries: Volume 4

T V SMITH

Published 2013 by arima publishing

www.arimapublishing.com

ISBN 978 1 84549 600 5

© T V Smith 2013

Printed and bound in the United Kingdom

arima publishing
ASK House, Northgate Avenue
Bury St Edmunds, Suffolk IP32 6BB
t: (+44) 01284 700321

www.arimapublishing.com

ACKNOWLEDGEMENT

Thanks to everyone who unwittingly became a
character in this book, and to those whose photos
I used in it: Kalle Sipilä, Ella Ruohonen,
Tommi Tornivaara (Finland), Blabla nurse AKO,
Satoshi Kurokawa (Japan). The rest I took myself.
That's why they're out of focus.

CONTENTS:

1. TVOM! (2009)

<u>5th January</u>

Two weeks in Germany teaming up with my mate Vom on drums for a tour as a duo. I'll be flying over to Düsseldorf a day early so we can have a rehearsal and get the van we're borrowing from friends ready. They've warned us that it's on its last legs and there's a good chance it won't get through the whole tour. It doesn't even have winter tyres fitted. When I looked up the weather for Düsseldorf last night, the low was forecast as minus thirteen.

There is sleet in the air and an icy wind as I wait for the Heathrow train at Acton Town station. A bow-legged elderly Irishman homes in on me and points at the guitar.

'A musician are you? What kind of music da ye play?'

I decide to hedge my bets. 'Sort of…rock.'

'Ahhh. 'Cos there's a mate of mine runs a pub. He's lookin' for musicians. Brings in the punters. I was down there last night. This woman got to talking to me and asked if I was married, I told her I don't rightly know meself. I asked her if she was and she said, no but she has four kids. *Bejayzus*, too much baggage I told her. Anyways, I play an instrument, you know – accordion. A beauty. Cost two hundred pounds from a boot sale. Weighs a fockin' ton. I don't play any more though. Got pissed one night in the pub and smashed the cunt. What's your favourite music then? The Who, is it?'

'Well, I liked them.'

'Local boys. Shepherds Bush. Ever heard of Matt Monroe? He was a local boy too. Turnham Green, used to work on the buses. Drank down the Crown And Sceptre. They said he could have been the next Nat King Cole. *When I faaaall in love….it will beee for evuuurrrrr…*'

He follows me on to the train. 'Music keeps you young though, eh? Look at me, I'm 68!'

A message from Vom comes through on the mobile. *Fucking hell, ten tons of snow fell last night. Good luck getting here…*

Here we go.

<u>6th January</u>

There was too much snow to get the car out of the garage last night so we couldn't go to rehearse, but ended up going downstairs to Vom's basement bar and rehearsing for the after-shows instead. We had something to celebrate: Vom's friend Micha has offered to lend us his brand new van for the tour – spacious, comfortable, and already fitted with winter tyres. It's a big relief.

Micha arrives with the van late afternoon and shows the controls to Herbie, who will be driving us and doing the merchandising. Herbie sits in the driver's seat gazing around him in awe and confusion at the panels and buttons. 'It's like an aircraft cockpit!' he gasps. Vom's wife Mary brings out a stack of towels from the house which we lay over the brand new carpets in the van, and Micha demonstrates how to kick the snow off our shoes before we get in. Then we head off to Cologne for the first gig of the tour. Somewhere along the way Herbie figures out how to work the heaters and windscreen wipers.

A quick run through a few songs in soundcheck and we're feeling confident. We sit in the freezing upstairs dressing room while the club fills below, the excitement mounting. Suddenly Vom's phone rings. He answers, and I see his jaw drop. He jumps to his feet. '*No!* OH NO!' he shouts.

The news is that his friend Manfred, the head of security for his regular band the Toten Hosen has died. They've just got back from a seven week tour together. Diagnosed with lung cancer a couple of years ago, Manfred had been undergoing treatment and seemed to be in remission until recently, when the cancer showed signs of returning. Not the kind of person to give in, he was preparing for another round of treatment but then dropped dead outside his house yesterday.

An hour to go before we're supposed to start and Vom is inconsolable.

But the show must go on. Our friend Pascal, who's travelling with us on the tour to play support, tells us that we're only ten people short of a sell out, then goes downstairs to play his set. Never mind rehearsal, Vom and I haven't even worked out a setlist yet. We find an old poster to write it out on, and Vom tries to drown his sorrows with a few vodkas as he scribbles out the names of the songs. Half an hour later, with a bit of alcohol-induced distance from the bad news, he's as ready as he's ever going to be so we head down the stairs, squeeze our way along behind the bar and through the packed audience and climb up on the stage. There's no such thing as a big rock'n'roll entrance in this kind of venue. We look out over the heads of the expectant crowd and Vom leans over to me. 'Er – I left the setlist upstairs.'

I battle my way back to get it while he adjusts the kit, up the stairs then back through the crowd, and finally we're ready to start. We have a great first gig of the tour. Afterwards we impress the promoter whilst working out the money in the office when Vom suddenly has to run out of the room to throw up. I had a suspicion that might happen when I heard him burp and then noticed him eyeing up the waste-paper bin.

Then it's time to load out into the van. I ask Vom why he has a label marked 'Vom #6' on his bag, and he explains that he forgets his bag so often that the Toten Hosen have made up numbered tags for him so that they can be counted in and out every night.

7th January

A long drive North to Hamburg, where we arrive at the *Hafenklang* late afternoon. The club is situated in a pedestrian area so Herbie has to negotiate the van between bollards and over the icy pavement to it – it's a tight squeeze and it occurs to me that if Micha could see this manoeuvre he'd probably take back the offer of lending us the van. We unload with a watchful eye out for traffic wardens.

I've played at the *Hafenklang* before and really liked the place but was disgusted by the sleeping quarters they provide around the corner: a large, cold basement room smelling of cat piss, with no water in the shower. There was a hose attached to one of the taps in the sink, and it was just about long enough to reach into the shower booth, but it only dispensed cold water. Curious as to what was behind the high screen dividing the washroom in half, I stood on a chair and peeked over to find a long-disused toilet block, seemingly once part of a club. I don't have the words to describe how dirty it was.

So anyway, it was a relief when a couple of days ago the venue contacted us to say that they won't inflict that room on us in this cold weather and are going to put us in a hotel.

The rock'n'roll hotel down near the harbour: not exactly luxury either, but comfortable, clean – and downstairs there's a bar that opens until the last customer has gone. That will probably be us. After a very enjoyable gig we pick up our keys and drop off our bags before heading down to make the most of it. In my little room the bed is on a platform four feet off the floor with the radiator underneath. I duck under there and switch the heat up to full, but when I get back from the bar a couple of hours later the room is still freezing. The only warm spot is the area under the platform, which has served as a heat trap. I consider staying under there but it seems ridiculous to sleep on the floor just like the bad old days of touring when I've actually got a hotel room. Instead it's a night with the socks on.

8th January

On the way to Flensburg Vom gets on the phone to the Toten Hosen office to organise how he can get to Manfred's funeral next week and still make it to our gig in Halle the same evening. Looks like he's going to have to get up at around 6:00 am in München to catch the 8:00 am flight to Frankfurt, then he'll be driven out to the little town where the funeral will take place. He'll be able to spend about an hour there before having to get back to Frankfurt railway station for the train to Halle. If everything works out he'll get to the venue just in time for soundcheck.

We're in Flensburg in good time and have almost an hour before we need to get to the club so first we go to check in to the hotel. To my relief it's a pretty good one. I switch on the telly to a news channel which shows endless shots of cars crashing in the snow and informs me that you have to be an idiot to attempt to drive in this weather. Last night in Bavaria they recorded a temperature of minus 34.6.

We'll be there next week!

We meet downstairs to drive to the venue. Everything's great about the place: a lovely room with good stage and PA system in a stylishly renovated building that once housed a swimming pool; upstairs is a spacious dressing room with a large buffet laid out, and the people working here also offer to cook us a meal after the show.

'Isn't this great, it's all going really well!' Vom says, and then we exchange a worried glance:

Too well…

I'm caught by surprise when I start singing in soundcheck and find that my voice has almost completely gone. I have to break off and go to the dressing room to drink some throat tea, but when I get back it's no better. I don't have a sore throat, and my speaking voice is normal, but when I try and sing, all that comes out is a tuneless wheeze.

It's all very worrying, but the show must go on. Feeling very despondent, I go upstairs and boil a kettle for another cup of throat tea, then scald my finger as I pour it out. It's only the hand I play guitar with!

We head downstairs to check out how many people are in. Looks like only about forty. Vom groans, but I'm secretly pleased: less people to embarrass myself in front of. I still have no idea if I'm going to be able to sing at all.

We work out a setlist of the songs that aren't going to be too much of a strain on my voice then pace around the dressing room while Pascal goes down to start his set. Vom peers through the window hoping to see more people arriving. 'There's a taxi, he's pulling up….no, he's gone straight on! Hang on, here comes another one…he's gone past too. The fuckin' taxi drivers are taunting us!'

I wander over to the window too. 'There's another one,' I point out. 'Ah. He's taking someone away.'

I have another look downstairs, and see a few more people have arrived, many of them young kids wearing Toten Hosen T-shirts, but there are still large empty areas on the floor in front of the stage. I've never played Flensburg before, and no one seems to recognise me as I wander around. When I get back upstairs Vom says, 'You're not going to believe this. I was looking out and saw a couple of geezers who looked like they might be coming in. Then one of them spotted me at the window, stuck his tongue out, flicked me the "V"s and then they walked off!'

As we start the set I'm in a state of panic about whether I'm going to be able to get through the next 90 minutes. For the first ten minutes my voice is atrocious, rasping below the note or suddenly squawking above it but never actually landing where I want it to go. Then as it warms up I find I can control it better, and for the last hour of the set it's almost normal. There are plenty of people in and they are dancing and singing along and clearly having a great time.

After the show Vom and I hang around downstairs chatting to the audience, but I notice that my speaking voice is rapidly disappearing. I escape upstairs to the dressing room, away from the crowds and noise, and soon I can't speak at all so I have to resort to whispering. I can still whisper perfectly. Soon everyone else in the room is whispering back, which gives the conversations an inappropriately intimate feel – particularly when we're working out the money. 'Do you always do it like this?' whispers the promoter.

9th January

The first thing I did when I woke up was try to speak, but absolutely nothing came out. I couldn't even make a noise when I gargled. Now I'm hanging over a sink of steaming hot water with a towel over my head, trying to force out a few test phrases for when I meet the others. I can't help wondering how much the sound carries down these pipes though: perhaps at this very moment there's someone in another room in the hotel cleaning his teeth and hearing a ghastly rasping voice floating out of the plughole: *one, two…one, two…we could cancel now…or we could go to Erfurt and see what happens…one, two…*

At twelve we drive back out to the club to pick up the gear. The soundman is sitting at the bar taking a break from tidying the place up, and in something between a whisper and a bark I ask him if there's a pharmacy nearby. He gives me some directions and also tells me that he is in a band and his singer swears by a particular throat lozenge that *always* works – he'll just pop over to his apartment and get some. He returns with the last couple left in the tin. From what I can translate, they seem to be made out of pansies.

At the pharmacy, I increase my armoury with the addition of some *Bad Emser* mineral salts tablets and a huge bottle of fennel honey. Then we hit the road: a four hour drive ahead of us to Erfurt.

At the first rest stop we make I stand at the coffee machine trying to figure out how it works and a guy working behind the counter comes over to help. 'You sound like a Londoner,' he says – (lucky he didn't hear me an hour ago) – 'I'm from Battersea, how about you?'

'West London,' I say. 'How come you're over here?'

'Army,' he says. 'They said, *join the army and see the world* – I joined the army and ended up working in a petrol station on the motorway.'

Many hours later and we leave the autobahn onto the minor roads as dusk starts to fall. Sunset, the landscape like a wedding cake, we watch the temperature on the dashboard readout drop minute by minute until it reaches minus fifteen.

The venue is a stone cellar down a long steep stairway which means a difficult load-in. The stage has a large pillar in front of it right in the middle so Vom and I have to set up on either side. The audience on one side of the room will only be able to see Vom and those on the other side will only be able to see me. It's a wide stage and we seem a long way away from each other. There is a DJ booth behind me with a large parasol over it which makes it look like an ice cream kiosk.

To my relief, thanks to generous amounts of pansy tablets and fennel honey my voice has returned enough to sing in soundcheck and I feel pretty sure I'll be able to get through the gig, even if it's not going to be the best ever. We sit in the freezing dressing room while the audience comes in and every now and then I go out to see how things are looking. There are an awful lot of people with Toten Hosen T-shirts, and when we eventually get on stage there are considerably more people on Vom's side of the room than mine.

My voice is fine for the gig, but ten minutes after I finish singing it completely disappears again. While the rest of our party go out into the club to meet the audience and have fun I sit in the dressing room for the next three hours, bundled up in two coats and a scarf against the cold, miserable and worrying about my voice, seriously contemplating the idea that I might have to cancel the tour.

Finally everyone else is ready and we heave the equipment up the stairs and load the van, our breath hanging over us in clouds. The hostel we're booked into is just a short drive away and we hurriedly park and head across the road to it, keen to get out of the cold. All I can think about now is getting some sleep and giving my voice some time to recover.

It's not that simple. The promoter gave us three sets of keys, each with four keys on them, but none of them fit the door. It seems to take forever to try them all, while our extremities go numb in the sub-zero temperatures. Finally, repeated ringing of the bell brings a puzzled '*Hallo?*' from the loudspeaker by the door. We explain our predicament. '*Oh Scheisse! Ha ha, oh Scheisse!*' comes the disembodied voice.

Scheisse indeed. The night entrance is around the corner.

10th January

It's eight in the morning and I could still get another three hours sleep, but the call of the bladder is too great. Unfortunately the rooms aren't en suite, so I put on a pair of shorts then step out of the room and start to shuffle up the corridor to look for the toilet. At that moment a woman comes out of the room opposite, smartly dressed in full winter clothing and apparently heading down to Reception to check out. She looks me up and down.

'*Guten Morgen*,' she says, tentatively.

'*Guten Morgen*,' I whisper back.

We gather at midday and set off for tonight's gig in Schwäbisch Gmund, an uneventful drive except for the moment when a huge buzzard, paralysed with the cold, tumbles out of the sky and crashes down onto the road in front of the van.

I'd never heard of Schwäbisch Gmund before, but sure enough there's a little music club here and we get a warm welcome from the young people running it as we pull up. Everyone helps unload the van, and there are snacks and drinks laid out on the dressing room table. The only downside is that the PA equipment is simply not up to scratch and it's impossible to hear what I'm singing in soundcheck. This is the one thing I do not need right now: my voice is still weak, and ninety minutes straining tonight could do some serious damage. The engineer apologises and explains that the club just doesn't have the money to service the equipment so a lot of it doesn't work. In the end we stack one of the monitor boxes on top of some other cabinets so it's just a few inches from my head and functions like one side of a large pair of bad quality earphones.

Despite the problems, the good thing about clubs like this is that everyone's glad you came so there's a great atmosphere in the room when we play and it's a really enjoyable gig. A lot of people have traveled a long way despite the weather just out of curiosity to see what a gig in Schwäbisch Gmund could be like. The sound is even okay once we start and I still have a voice when we finish, which is a huge relief. The worst might be over. Afterwards there are a lot of autographs to be signed and the hospitality flows so that by the time Vom and I are called into the office to work out the money we're not really in a fit state. We spend quite some time in there. There is a lot of crashing around and laughing. At one point Vom is in a shopping trolley carrying the wad of cash the promoter has just handed him clamped between his teeth. After a while I step out of the office to find a dressing room full of people with concerned looks on their faces.

'What is going on in there?' asks Pascal.

'Oh, we're just working out the money,' I say. 'It's a good one!'

Then it's time to leave. One of the two brothers who promoted the gig is sober and is going to drive us over to his parents' place in a village nearby, where we'll have the top floor of the house to ourselves. We'll come back and pick up the van and our gear tomorrow morning. The ground outside is ultra-slippery and it's a miracle no one falls over on the way to the car considering how unsteady on our feet most of us are. Perhaps Vom is a bit more unsteady than most, I think, as he throws his bag into the boot and then attempts to climb in after it. When we are all safely installed and on the road I can hear him slurring to Pascal, '*Who* is that bloke in the front?'

It's me.

11th January

I go downstairs, where the parents point me to the shower and then sit down with me at the loaded breakfast table. Slowly the rest of our party arrive and fuel up, Vom impressively undamaged from last night's excesses. The parents show us the photo of me and him in the local paper, and tell us that Grandma saw it and pointed at Vom and said, what a nice looking girl!

Tonight we're playing in a tiny club in Karlsruhe, perhaps the smallest on the tour so far but there's a feeling that with a full room it could be a good one. The dressing room is a bone-freezing concrete storeroom at the front of the club – hardly good for getting you in the mood to play, but the gig is a sweaty, heaving success, the best of the tour so far.

Afterwards we relax with the last remaining members of the audience, having a few beers while old punk records play on the decks. A guy points at the bottle I am holding. 'This beer is well known because the brewery is right next to a cemetery. The water flows beneath the graveyard, which is supposed to give it its special taste.'

Fascinating. I switch to wine. And that's why when we're all singing along to 'Hurry Up Harry' later I'm the only one holding a thin-stemmed wine glass aloft to the *We're going daaahn the pub* line.

12th January

Pascal and Vom were sharing a room last night. Pascal tells me that he woke up at some point and heard Vom get up to use the toilet. He didn't come back for a long while, and then Pascal heard a distant knocking noise. He got up to see what was going on and found Vom up the corridor knocking on the door to someone else's room. Lucky they didn't open it.

In the van, Vom passes around some religious pamphlets that were forced on him by a woman at the gig last night. He's not sure why she homed in on him to convert, but the cartoon-style pamphlets give us a good laugh and help pass the time. The characters act out morality tales to demonstrate how sinful behaviour will damn you to hell, and they swear a lot. 'Bunk!' they say. I think we may be saying 'bunk' quite a lot on the rest of this tour. In one picture a man ogles a woman walking past, with a thought balloon over his head saying, 'Mmm, nice!' He's going down.

Somewhere on the trip to Regensburg we stop at a service station, something we usually try and avoid in Bavaria because anyone who looks even slightly out of the ordinary is liable to be hauled over by the borderline-fascist Bavarian police. I'm ordering a coffee when Vom comes back from the toilets. 'Still had the Sat Nav on in my pocket,' he says. 'This voice was coming out – *turn left in one hundred metres.* Bloke next to me gave me a funny look.'

We arrive in Regensburg to find a big welcome from the promoter Stefan, a well-run large club with a good sound system and a dressing room with food and drink laid out for us. The club fills up rapidly and my voice is pretty much back to normal so I'm looking forward to this even though the fatigue is seriously kicking in. I'm not the only one – just before we get on stage Vom says, 'I'll be able to take the beers up in the bags under my eyes.'

We're in top form for the show and afterwards it seems that most of the audience want to talk to us. By the time they've all gone home none us are really in a fit state to work out the money. We sit down with Stefan in the dressing room and go over and over the figures but they don't add up. Meanwhile we're missing the chance to catch up on some much-needed sleep so after an hour of increasing frustration, not to mention boredom, we agree to come back and sort it out tomorrow.

Now there's just a short drive to the hotel. It's slightly worrying that Herbie has noticed a bulb in one of the headlamps isn't working – reason enough for the Bavarian police to throw us in jail for six years – but no, we're renegades, we're *breakin' the law, breakin' the law*, and we get to the hotel without being captured and instead have a nice sleep.

13th January

The bottles of water lying around in the back of the van have frozen solid.

Back to the club, but daylight doesn't throw much light on the issue of the money. It's all very confusing, and requires multiple trips by Stefan up to the office to get receipts and tallies of the amount of people who came in last night, including figures of how many bought tickets in advance, how many at the door, percentages against guarantee, V.A.T., foreign artist tax…oh, it's all too much before breakfast.

Finally, armed with a sheet of paper full of incomprehensible scribblings and an as-good-as-it-gets approximation of what we earned, we are ready to leave. At last we can forget the money issue and thank Stefan for what was actually a wonderful night and a great gig.

Now we have a long drive to Vienna ahead of us, but before we leave we have to get that headlamp fixed. We phone up Micha to tell him the bad news, and he says he's sorry but it's a specialist job and we're going to have to find the correct car dealer to get it done. He's loaned us his van for free and he's apologising! The good news is, it turns out there's a dealership on the outskirts of town, but as we pull up in front of the smart offices and men in spotless pressed dungarees home in on the open bonnet, Vom and I can see last night's profits – whatever they were – evaporating before our eyes.

Q. How many Bavarians does it take to change a car lightbulb?

A. One. And even though it takes him nearly an hour he only charges us eleven euros. We're punching air as we leave.

With all that drama going on there was no time for breakfast so the first thing we do when we hit the motorway is stop off to fill up the van with petrol and ourselves with coffee. I head off to the café and look back to see Herbie and Vom at the pumps being questioned by the police – caught in the act of refuelling whilst in possession of dyed hair, technically a crime in Bavaria. After we're all back in the van and on the road again, Vom tells me that they started off asking for his identity card then when they realised who he was ended up asking for his autograph.

It's been years since I last played at the Chelsea club in Vienna, and walking in again today feels like coming home. As soon as you get through the door you know it's going to be a great gig. The only problem, club manager Othmar tells me, is that the usual soundman is ill, so he had to get a replacement. Unfortunately the replacement soundman got ill too, so tonight we have the replacement replacement soundman who's never worked here before. Soundcheck takes quite a long time. After that there's just time for Herbie to drive me over to the hotel to check in and freshen up before the gig. In a state of extreme fatigue I accidentally cut my fingernail too close and it's so painful I can hardly hold a plectrum.

Yes, we have been on tour a thousand years and are very tired. Upstairs in the tiny Chelsea dressing room, Vom and I keep having manic laughter attacks as I attempt to bandage my finger with electrical tape and he attempts to write out his setlist and song intro cues on the back of a poster.

'Er, what's the next one?' he says, felt pen in hand, 'Oh, yes, the German song – *Es Stört Mich Nicht*…that's a 1-2-3-4 count in, isn't it?'

I look at what he's written: *Es Blobb ich nich 1,3,*

14th January

I wake up to find snow swirling down outside the window. It's lying thick and slushy on the roads and the Vienna traffic has slowed to a crawl. We have to get back to Bavaria today – good job we've got those winter tyres.

My friend PamP from Garden Gang is going to sing *Es Blobb ich nich* with us tonight in Münich so we have a quick run-through at soundcheck, then I go over to the radio studio in an adjacent building to record an interview and song for the weekly programme he's recently started presenting. Pascal comes too, and brings his accordion to join in on 'The Day We Caught The Big Fish.' Although it's one of my easiest songs to sing I'm struggling with finding enough energy to get through it, all my limbs are aching and it's hard to concentrate. Definitely get the feeling I'm going down with some kind of flu, probably the one Pascal was just getting over when we started the tour. That would explain the problem with the voice a few days ago.

Next door, in the rooms provided for the bands to stay overnight, it's clear that Vom's not too healthy either. From one of the bedrooms I can hear him coughing and groaning, and when he emerges half an hour before stage time he says he feels terrible. To make it worse, tomorrow is Manfred's funeral and he's going to have to get up before dawn to catch the flight.

Fired up by a packed and lively audience we forget about being ill while on stage and have a great gig. Then I leave Vom, Pascal and Herbie to it, and take a lift with PamP back to his home in Markt Indersdorf. Time for a break from my touring party, a chance to catch up with an old friend, a little something to eat, a couple of *Dunkelweizen* beers and sleep.

15th January

After a good breakfast I'm feeling vaguely fit again by the time PamP drives me back to the club, where Herbie and Pascal have just finished packing the van. To my surprise – call me a cynic – they tell me Vom actually got up in time for the taxi.

Now it's a long, long drive to the next gig in Halle. Without Vom around, the mood in the van is more laid back. Herbie fixes his attention on the road, and Pascal and I are too tired to do more than exchange a few words. Over the next five hours we get SMS updates from Vom: he's made it to the funeral, he's caught the train to Halle, he's waiting in the hotel.

It's dark and late by the time we arrive. It takes some time to find the venue, which is located in a medieval tower. We have to drive along what used to be the moat to get to the door to load in. Carrying the gear through the deep snow and up a narrow iron staircase is filled with potential hazards – God knows what it will be like at the end of the night – but everyone from the club pitches in to help. Despite the fact we're late the sound crew don't have everything set up yet. It's nearly time for doors to open but there's no sense of urgency and soundcheck is methodical and slow. It's a small PA system for the size of the room and it's hard to hear what's going on. My finger is so painful I can hardly play guitar. I find myself thinking: just get through this. Only three gigs to go.

16th January

I know I'm over-tired when I can't find my room key, even though I evidently got into the room last night with it. Still, it gives the girls working at the hotel an interesting ten minutes as they watch me unload my suitcase in front of the reception desk and spread everything out across the floor. I eventually find the key in my bag of dirty laundry.

On the road to Wilhemshaven, way up in the North, we get a phone call to tell us that the final gig of the tour in Ratingen has already sold out, which is cheering news. But first there's tonight and tomorrow to get through and I'm a bit apprehensive about tonight. A guy called Tim is putting on the gig to celebrate his birthday, and holding it in the large warehouse where he lives. Vom's played the place before with his band Spitting Vicars and assures me it's going to be fun, but I'm nervous about it: I've never played in Wilhelmshaven before and to make it worse this flu is showing no signs of going away. I'm feeling weak and dizzy, and hardly likely to give the best performance of my life tonight.

Meantime, there's the issue of getting a few birthday presents for Tim, and the only opportunity we have to shop is at the motorway service station. As Tim has a rather striking moustache, Vom buys him a can of shaving foam and a pack of disposable razors. Herbie selects a glossy magazine called 'Cats' with a cute photo of some cats on the cover.

'Is Tim a cat lover then?' I ask.

Herbie shrugs his shoulders. 'I don't know.'

We arrive in Willhemshaven late afternoon and for the first time on this tour there's no snow on the ground. The temperature has soared to just above freezing, but there's a chill wind blowing down from the North coast. Tim welcomes us in and takes us up to his flat on the first floor, then on to the top floor of the building, a large concrete-floored room where the bands will play. At the moment his fourteen year old son is practicing up there with his band – they'll be supporting us tonight and it will be their first ever gig. Back downstairs the first few people for the party are already starting to turn up. The plan is that Vom and Pascal will sleep in a room next to the living room tonight, but that looks like it will get very noisy later so I'm glad that me and Herbie are going to get rooms in the hotel over the road. I go there to check in now and when I get to the room to drop off my bag I have to fight to resist the temptation to lie down and go to sleep for a year.

Back at the venue the young band have finished rehearsals and it's time for Vom and me to soundcheck, but the soundman has gone. The gig is supposed to start in an hour and I really would like to make sure everything is working but my attempts to plug in my guitar result in a hideous squealing, the kind that suggests the P.A. system will shortly explode. I feel my mood plummet, give up and go and sit downstairs while Tim phones around to try and get the soundman back. I'm afraid I might have damaged my ears – I keep thinking I can hear a persistent high-pitched peeping sound. No, hang on, I really *can* hear it: I check in my bag and find my alarm clock is going off. But I still can't wake up.

Tim is good-naturedly fielding complaints from his son that we have changed all the settings on the desk when we tried to do our soundcheck, just after they had it all set up perfectly for their band. Welcome to the world of rock'n'roll, son – it will only get worse.

Not as many people have arrived at the party as expected by the time the young band start their set. About forty gather in front of them as they get into their first song, a lot of people I know who've travelled up from Düsseldorf, friends of Tim, and a few paying guests. The kids do a great job for their first gig and come offstage flushed and excited, which only makes me feel sicker and more tired than I already am. Pascal, nervous about playing in front of this audience, cuts down his solo set to just a couple of songs, then it's time for Vom and me. Just before we start, Tim gets a phone call to say that a popular punk band called The Mimmis have just arrived and have offered to spontaneously play a set for him. As we have a 10:00 curfew because of the neighbours that means Vom and I should cut down our set to forty minutes. Secretly I'm relieved.

The sound from the stage monitors is atrocious and neither of us can hear any guitar or vocals in them. But before we know it we're on the last number, and then Tim is up at the microphone to thank us, announce the Mimmis and have the inevitable 'Happy Birthday' sung to him. At that moment, Herbie arrives with the hastily-wrapped presents. Full of curiosity Tim strips off the paper and pulls out the razors and shaving foam. He turns slowly round to Vom who is ducking down behind the drum kit.

'You…you….you *bunking bunk*!' he exclaims.*

(*Those aren't the actual words he used.)

Then the Mimmis play, I can relax with a beer, which helps take the edge off the flu, and downstairs the party kicks into life. At one point I'm chatting with Herbie and Pascal, wondering where Vom has got to, when he suddenly appears in the doorway wearing an old car tyre he's found somewhere around his neck.

'I'm tired,' he says.

Me too, and now sleep is more important than the party. Still two days to get through. Herbie looks like he has been put through the wringer as well and we both decide to leave everyone else to it and go back to the hotel.

Back in the superheated hotel room – they don't seem to have adjusted their thermostat to the change in the weather – I gratefully strip off my stage clothes and fill the basin in the bathroom. Water seeps out from somewhere around the basin edge and gradually floods the shelf and flows over onto the floor. I switch the taps off, throw a towel down and hope that will stop it. *Punk star mysteriously drowns in night! On third floor!*

I'm desperately thirsty, so just before I go to sleep I risk the bathroom again to get a glass of water, but when I run the cold tap – sparking off another mini-flood – all that comes out is hot water. I give up.

17th January

I wake up feeling like I haven't been to sleep. Ever.

Over at Tim's flat a few people are awake, shellshocked expressions on their faces, including Tim who is wearing a dashing white Stetson and clearly hasn't slept. Everywhere there are empty bottles lying around, the kitchen is full of unwashed dishes and glasses, and in the office area there is a broken television tipped up on the floor.

'What happened there?' I ask Tim.

He looks at it and strokes his chin thoughtfully. 'Hmm, I don't really know why that thing is standing on its head myself,' he says. He doesn't seem too bothered about it.

When everyone is awake we hit the road. Hours later, as we pull up to the venue, tucked away in a courtyard of an Aachen backstreet, it occurs to me that this area looks familiar and I realise we're right opposite where my website manager Klaus used to live. I often stayed the night at his flat and I never even knew there was a venue over the road.

Turns out to be a nice place too: a large club and everyone pleased to see us. Soundcheck turns out to be a lengthy affair, though. For some reason there are two sound guys, each with their own mixing desk, and by the time they are both happy Vom and I are exhausted and there is just a short time left before we play. No time to relax or check in to the hotel, even though the promoter tells us it's a good one and just a short walk away.

Soon there's a good crowd in, the room is buzzing, and it's another great gig, despite the fact Vom and I feel like death two minutes before getting on stage. Too tired to go out and meet the audience after the show, we slump in the dressing room, soaked with sweat, aching, coughing and groaning. When most of the audience has gone, we decide against finding our way to the hotel by foot and get the promoter to call us a cab. Outside we find Klaus and a few other friends of ours waiting, hoping to entice us out for a drink in town, but we're literally on our last legs and have to leave them to it.

A good job we decided to go by cab: the hotel is further away and the route more complicated than we were led to believe. We would never have made it if we'd walked. We would have trudged around until we collapsed in the street, then got picked up by some roaming medical experimentation van and our bodies donated to germ research.

The bed in the hotel is the most beautiful thing I have seen in my life. And with just an hour to drive tomorrow I can spend ten hours in it! Life is sweet.

18th January

Driving back to Düsseldorf, all of us coughing and hacking away, Herbie mentions that we sound like what translates as 'the disease cave.' He sounds a bit blocked up himself but claims that he hasn't caught the cold, it's just that the air conditioning in the bus is rather fierce. I think he's in denial. In fact, the air conditioning unit has become the breeding ground for our germs and anyone who gets in this bus over the next six months will catch whatever it is we've got. Sorry about that, Micha.

We pass Vom's place on the way to Ratingen so we drop in. Mary has prepared a hot meal for us and we fall on it like people who haven't eaten for two weeks – not that far from the truth. A girl from BUT fanzine arrives to do a quick interview to accompany a book she's producing from the compiled back issues of the fanzine. We talk about how it was when I first spoke to her, ten years ago when I first started coming over to Germany and her fanzine was one of the only ones who paid any attention to me. I remember it all too well: in those days I didn't have any CDs out and the bag I brought on tour with me contained some clothes, a sleeping bag and – my luxury item – my own pillow. I knew virtually no one in Germany and at the end of the night I would often end up on a dirty mattress in some stranger's house. I remember the tiny venues where no one came and I didn't get paid. Unable to speak German, I spent hours not knowing what people where saying around me, drifting off while everyone else seemed to be having fun, far from home, lonely, disorientated.

But that was then. Now it's time to leave for tonight's – already sold out – gig, which I know will be full of familiar faces, people singing along and happy to see me: friends.

And so it is. And afterwards, climbing up the stairs to 'my' room in Vom's place, the skin peeling off the back of my hands from the kettle burn, fingernail bloody and stinging, aching, tired, ill, but with an intense sense of fulfilment and the satisfaction of a job well done – it occurs to me that even though this is not everybody's idea of success, it's all been worth it.

19th January

According to the experts, says the newspaper on my flight home, today – 19th January, 2009 – will be the most depressing day in history.

History is bunk.

Vom!

Herbie!

2. OSCAR MATERIAL (2009)

24th March

What am I walking into? Last year when I played Finland, my tour agent Harri picked me up from Helsinki airport, something he'd never done before, and after half an hour of small talk during the drive to the first gig in Tampere, he got to the point.

'Tim, you know that I teach a college course about the music business. I was wondering if perhaps your next tour here could be organised by my students.'

It would give them an invaluable experience of real life touring, he reckoned. I said yes.

Then a few weeks ago I heard from a film maker at the same college who asked if he could make a documentary about the tour. I said yes to that too. After all, if you're going to have a catastrophe you might as well get it all down for posterity.

On the plane there is an English-language Helsinki newspaper in my seat pocket, and a couple of items in it catch my eye. First, there's an article about an increase in incidents of Malaria in Finnish tourists coming back from tropical countries – presumably they're so used to having swarms of mosquitoes at home that they don't think twice about protecting themselves when they're abroad. Second: Finland is seeing an increase in incidents of Vole Fever. The professor of the Forest Research Institute says: 'We've received calls from people reporting sightings of field voles staggering in the snowdrifts…'

Glad I brought my camera.

It's a long nervous wait for the guitar to come up on the baggage carousel, but when I finally have that and my suitcase I head out into the Arrivals hall to look for Teemu, the student who will be my tour manager for the next five days. I don't usually have a tour manager but, hey, if it helps someone learn something and makes my life easier, I'm not complaining. It doesn't take long to spot him. A young guy raises his arm as I come through the doors, and sure enough, either side of him there are two cameramen with their lenses trained on me, as well as a guy holding a long boom microphone high over their heads. Teemu steps forward and one of the cameramen breaks away from the pack and scuttles after him with a hand-held, the sound guy following close behind. I'm resolutely trying to ignore the cameras so that the film looks authentic but probably they catch my idiotic double-take as I gawp at Teemu's moustache, which has Dali-esque curls at the sides but is shaved bare in the middle. For a moment I think he is wearing a fake one for some reason to do with the film that I've not been told about. But no, it's real, and I recover quickly to say 'Hello, you must be Teemu,' very natural, positively Oscar material. Teemu shakes my hand and says we are a bit late and should get going straight away, so we hurry out to the bus, leaving the camera crew in the arrivals lounge. They've just got some of the most boring footage ever committed to celluloid.

Once we're round the corner and out of sight I say to Teemu, 'I hope they think that was worth it. It's not going to get any more interesting than that.'

As soon as we cross the road the bus for Helsinki pulls up and we board it, catching the camera crew on the hop so they have to run after us still packing away their gear. On the trip into the city we get the chance to introduce ourselves. There's the director and camera operator Kalle – he's the one who's been emailing me – then Rene, who is filming with the hand-held camera, and Juho who is recording the sound. They're all very friendly, and mercifully have a good sense of humour: as they hoist up their cameras again when we arrive at Helsinki railway station, I say: 'From now on I'm going to ignore you. It won't be difficult,' and they laugh.

So the crew trail Teemu and me into the railway station, and when we go into the booking office they call us back to go through the door a second time because they missed it. There's probably going to be a lot of that sort of thing over the next few days.

On the train there's an exchange of seating places with other passengers so that Teemu and I can sit opposite each other and the crew can set up the tripod in the gangway and capture us both as we go through the schedule for the tour. It's a weird feeling, knowing everything you say and do is being recorded: instead of just acting normally, you actually have to try and act normally.

When we've finished with the schedule, we leaf through a couple of newspapers that are lying on the table in front of us in an attempt to not look too boring. Teemu reads out a fascinating fact: 'It says here that if you get ill, you should microwave your toothbrush afterwards to prevent getting re-infected.'

'I don't have a microwave,' I say. 'Would the ordinary oven be alright?'

Eventually the crew put the cameras down again and I go up to the buffet car and drink a coffee with them. They tell me that in order to get the shot of me coming out of the doors at Immigration in the airport they had to set up as soon as they heard the plane had landed, then for thirty minutes while I was inside waiting for my luggage they filmed everyone who came through the door, never knowing which one was going to be me.

We arrive in Turku, and capture the *getting-off-the-train-and-carrying-all-the-gear-through-the-snow-to-the-gig* sequence. When I left London this morning it was warm Spring weather and my bag was so heavy with CDs to sell at the gigs that I almost decided to ditch the winter clothing and lighten my load – now I'm glad that I didn't. It's punishingly cold here.

The Klubi is a nice-looking venue. The support band is already on stage soundchecking when I walk in and it seems like the sound system is a good one. When Teemu first emailed me the name of the supports for the first two dates of the tour – Anssi 8000 and Maria Stereo – I assumed it was two bands, but it turns out to be a duo. Very charming too – a husband and wife band: he plays guitar and sings and also has a kick drum and snare with a specially adapted pedal set up in front of him so that he can play both of them with his feet; she sings, plays keyboards with one hand and the rest of the drum kit, cymbals and hi-hat, with the other.

My soundcheck goes quickly then I slip off to check in to my hotel, a Holiday Inn just a five minute walk away. Better than my normal standard of hotel – maybe they're trying to make me look classy for the film. If so, I'm not complaining.

I drop off my bag and get back to the venue. Tuesday night in Turku, and only about twenty people in when Anssi and Maria start their set. I'm thinking, this is going to look really embarrassing on the film, but people steadily come in and by the time I'm supposed to play the place is comfortably full. On the way to the stage I stop by the merchandise table that Teemu is manning and suddenly loads of people come up and start buying CDs and asking me to sign them. They don't even seem put off by the cameras hovering inches from their faces. I'm in a good mood by the time I get away and on stage, twenty minutes later than intended. Afterwards people gather around the table again and I have to politely ask them to stop buying stuff because I need it for the rest of the tour.

Soon the audience has gone, the film crew pack up, Teemu heads off to stay the night with a friend of his, and I'm left alone in the dressing room with a drunken photographer who claims he works for the club and incessantly takes pictures of me. There really is no getting away from being on film on this tour.

I slip away as soon as I can, and on the way out I find the manager chatting with his girlfriend outside. An icy wind is whipping around them. The photographer has followed me up the stairs and continues to snap away. Clearly he isn't quite as much the official photographer as he claimed because as he darts around investigating good angles for shots he asks the manager if there is any chance of getting the job. The manager glances at the camera. 'Mmm, for a start I think you should remove *that*,' he says. The lens cap is still on.

The photographer goes off in disgrace, and I chat with the manager for a while, mentioning how quickly the gig emptied out after the show. Normal for a Tuesday, I suppose.

'For them, yes,' he says, 'but for us Tuesday is party night. They are the Normals. *They* only party at the weekend, but Tuesday is *our* night.'

Well, I wouldn't like to think of myself as a Normal, but I've got four gigs ahead of me and it's already got very late so I say my goodbyes and edge my way carefully along the ice-packed pavements back to the hotel, carrying my guitar and what's left of the merch, as well as the take-away falafel meal the club ordered in for me before the show, which of course I didn't want to eat then.

Probably I should have worn my gloves. After half an hour in the room I can feel my fingers again and am able to hold a fork and have a stab at the food. I eat half and leave the rest in the minibar for an emergency falafel breakfast.

25th March

How the heart wells up with joy to find that the plastic tray holding cups and sachets of coffee and tea has an *integral* socket for the kettle. You just plug in the tray. Admittedly, the switch on the kettle doesn't work so I have to stand there holding it down until it boils – opening the coffee sachet with my teeth and writing my emails with the other hand – while the time approaching midday checkout draws ever nearer. But all the same – *you plug in the whole tray.*

I leave my guitar and suitcase in the hotel luggage room and go out for a walk. When I get back just before one o'clock, Teemu and the camera crew are already in Reception, waiting to get clearance to go upstairs and film a room so they can make a montage of the hotels I'm staying in. People will think I stay in Holiday Inns all the time! Maybe this will lead to an improvement in my accommodation in future!

When they get back from the room we all head up the road to the railway station where we catch the train to Tampere. Desperate to give the crew something to film I reach up to the luggage rack to get my guitar case so that they can get the *TV-changes-strings-on-the-train* shot. As I lift it down I notice someone further down the carriage giving me a *who-is-this-guy-and-what's-so-special-about-him-that-he-has-a-camera-crew-filming-him* look.

In Tampere it's another Holiday Inn. I pick up a free booklet about the town on the way up to the room and am fascinated to see that there are a few more museums than last time I looked. For example, there's the Shoe Museum and the Refrigeration Museum.

At soundcheck, the film crew tell me they have a set-up organised for tonight – they want me to go to a pop quiz in a pub: I am to stand next to the quizmaster and his first question will be: who is this man? As embarrassing career moves go, this could be a few steps down from opening a supermarket. But without the fee. Unfortunately the pub quiz starts at around the same time as Anssi and Maria's set, which I really want to see, so Kalle phones up the guy asking the questions and arranges for him to have a run-through for the cameras earlier as no audience shots are required anyway. Time is going to be tight though, so we need to leave now.

I hurry down the streets of Tampere while the crew sprint around me, moving in close, falling back, continually interrupted by evening shoppers who want to know what they are filming. Then we hurry into the pub and quickly fake up the quiz. The guy asks the questions holding an unplugged microphone while I stand next to him acting bemused: easy because I actually am.

On the way back the crew decide to shoot me walking through the picturesque old town area by the river where factory buildings have been renovated into smart bars and shops. They bustle along behind me as I speed through the narrow dimly-lit cobbled alleyways and over the bridge. At one point I stop and lean over to gaze meaningfully at the black water rushing past below.

Afterwards, when Kalle has yelled *cut!* I tell him, 'That was a little idea of my own. It's Oscar material as long as you don't fuck it up in the edit.'

I shake the cameras off briefly and slip into a pub near the venue to meet up with Punk Lurex and some of their friends. I'm happy to hear that the band have decided to reform, although sad to hear that it will be without Riita, who is now happily settled in Seinajöke and can't really make the long trip down to Tampere for rehearsals. Still, it's great to meet Tiina and Kukka again, and they introduce me to their new guitarist, a 22 year old student. The same age as my tour manager! We're in the hands of babies!

The gig is a good one, but afterwards most of my friends seem a bit embarrassed about the film crew around me and soon disappear. The merch sales plunge to single figures. I pack away my guitar then sit in the downstairs dressing room and have a couple of beers with the film crew and accuse them of making me lose all my friends. They apologise, and then tell me about their experiences going along the street filming me earlier. A few people asked them if they were filming something for the police or a documentary about drug dealing. One drunk guy came up and got in front of the camera and said, 'My name is Poki. Are you making a film about me?'

They also tell me about a guy who owns lots of shopping centres in Finland and has decided to build a replica Titanic in Kliminki, a town in the middle of nowhere that has only 2,000 inhabitants. It's not even on the sea. Still, I'm thinking of going along with my replica iceberg.

26th March

A few hours break from being filmed this morning: Harri is picking me up from the hotel to take me and Teemu over to Virrat, the small town a couple of hours North from Tampere where he teaches, and where Teemu and the film crew study. It's really out in the wilds and no bands usually play there, but we're hoping for a decent turnout from the college. The crew are going to drive up in another car and meet us there.

It's nearly time for Harri's class by the time we arrive so he hurries off down the corridor and Teemu shows me the well-equipped sound studios used by the college. He's rehearsing in one of them this afternoon – his band will be supporting me tonight and it's their first gig. 'The guitarist has never even played with us before,' says Teemu. 'Actually, the plan is to have a new guitarist every gig.'

I leave them to it and wander back down the hill to my hotel room and after that ten minute walk feel I have seen just about all there is to see of Virrat. The hotel is a bit of a step down after the luxury of the last few days. The reception desk is closed and I seem to be the only person staying here. The room is spartanly furnished but with a cooker and fridge, and as there is no restaurant in the hotel the fridge has tomorrow's breakfast already installed: two small bread rolls, a chunk of cucumber and a tomato, as well as a plate with some slices of cheese and meat. Obviously the news about me being vegetarian hasn't reached Virrat.

I eat half the breakfast now. Luckily there's no UMM – well, it would be an EMM – because the meat hasn't actually touched the cheese, which is the processed type, shrink-wrapped in plastic and also tasting of it. Meanwhile, Teemu phones up to say that the venue has prepared some veggie balls to eat this evening, but – er – they put fish in them.

Kalle phones up, disappointed that he missed me looking round the college and suggests going over to his nearby flat for some coffee, he'll come by the hotel in half an hour. Apparently this is not strictly a social visit, because when the allotted time comes I look out of my second floor window and see Rene setting up the camera on the pavement opposite ready to capture me coming out of the front door.

Apparently Kalle is now going to be in the film because he comes up to meet me when I emerge. 'Do you like milk in your coffee?' he says. 'We could go and buy some milk.'

'I have some in my room – I'll pop back in and get that,' I say.

'No,' says Kalle, eyes flickering towards the camera, 'let's go and *buy some milk.*'

So we go round the corner to the supermarket, trailed closely by Rene and the camera, and Kalle buys some milk while I cast my eyes over the little toys and trinkets and unusual salty-liquorice sweets on display as if I am actually interested in them, and I've got to tell you it was Oscar material.

Kalle gets the coffee together in his kitchen while Rene films me leafing through a glossy photo book on Virrat, looking for ideas about what to do this afternoon.

'I've never walked on an ice lake before,' I say. 'Where is the nearest one?'

It's only a few hundred metres, down the other side of the hill from the college. On the way we decide to film some shots in my hotel for the hotel montage. I show off the remainder of my breakfast and Kalle takes care of the meat for me. He gets some footage of the empty corridors, murmuring approvingly about how they look like a prison block. He points at the number on my door, number three, then at the door next to mine, number one. 'Who is Number One?' he asks with a passable Patrick McGoohan impression.

'Probably Poki,' I say.

Soon after we are skidding down the path to the vast white expanse of the lake. I say, 'I wonder if there will be any ice fisherman. I'd like to see them making the hole with that drill-thing they use.'

'That's called a *kairata*,' says Kalle.

'A *kairata*?'

'*Kairata. Kairrrrrata.*'

I still have problems with those Finnish rolled 'r's. I practice the word a bit more, then realise what I am doing. 'Thank you,' I say, 'for teaching me a word I will *never* need again.'

We go down to the lake's edge where the summer jetties and diving platforms are locked into the ice. Kalle steps confidently off the bank and I follow him out towards the centre with a typical Englishman's concern that somehow this is wrong and must surely be dangerous. But the ice is solid as rock. The sun is just dipping below the tree-line, bathing the panorama in stark brilliance. There are no fisherman drilling holes but it's better without. Even the presence of the camera can't disturb the beauty and solitude of the place.

The venue tonight is a small bar called Club 66. I walk in just as Teemu's band finish their soundcheck, and he tells me that it went well but halfway through his Laney bass amp broke. There's a special mechanism in the cab that revolves to give a modulating effect to the sound, and the belt that drives it has snapped. He is going to try to repair it with curtain elastic.

There are some technical problems with my soundcheck so the crew get to film me looking bored for ages while the students run around checking cables and standing over the mixing desk with puzzled expressions until finally everything is working. There's no stage so the instruments and microphones are set up on the floor right in front of where the audience will be standing. Things could get chaotic later when the audience come in, but on the other hand it could lead to an exciting gig. Still a long time before show time though, so I go up to the little dressing room upstairs and sit down on the sofa there, not really knowing what to do with myself.

Kalle arrives upstairs, and looks at me. 'Everything okay?' he asks.

'Well, yes.' I say. 'It's just that there's still hours to go and there's nothing to do but hang around here trying not to get drunk.'

'That's hard to do in Virrat,' he says. 'Turn around and you're drunk.'

After a while I go back downstairs and watch the audience trickle in. I stand next to Trevor, a Yorkshireman who is teaching at the college and is also DJ for the evening. He points out one guy who is arguing with the doorman: 'He'll be thrown out by eleven. He always is.'

He tells me about how the logging companies have been drastically reducing their workforce recently. It's all being automated. After the trees have been felled, a probe is inserted into the logs, then a barcode is stuck on them that describes their size and moisture content. They're left by the road to be picked up, then taken off by lorry to the sawmills where the barcode is scanned and the logs stripped and cut into planks by computer-operated saws, no humans involved. The result is that the workers who used to live out in the forest have now come back into the towns. 'But there's nothing for them to do in a place like Virrat,' says Trevor, 'most of them don't last more than about four months before they drink themselves to death or commit suicide.'

I go back upstairs and am startled to find a black-robed hooded figure approaching me. But it's only Teemu, who neglected to tell me that his band perform in costume. They troop downstairs in their cloaks and play a half hour of prog-rock instrumentals with occasional vocoder, guitar and bass pounding away against a drum loop backing conducted by the keyboard player. I quite enjoy it, particularly as a contrast after Trevor's *Classic Driving Rock* CD, which he played earlier because he thought it would 'warm up the audience.'

My gig goes great, but when I unplug my guitar an hour later and wander over to the merchandising table no one buys anything. Bloody students.

Upstairs, Teemu introduces me to his girlfriend Nini, who plays in a Finnish girl band with a name I have trouble pronouncing when I read it off the CD – *Pintandwefall* – until she points out it's not Finnish, it's English: pint and we fall.

We get to talking about my walk on the lake and she tells me she just did a fashion shoot for a magazine cutting a hole out of an ice lake with a chainsaw.

A chainsaw? Why not a *kairata*?

Everyone seems to have gone so it's time to pack up and get back to the hotel. There's so much merch left that I have trouble fitting it all into my shoulder bag. I'm trudging along trying to keep upright on the icy pavements, weighed down by the guitar and bag, when I hear a vehicle slowing as it approaches. Thinking it might be a taxi, I lift my head hopefully and start to wave it down, only to find it's actually a police van. At that moment the cardboard box full of CDs in my shoulder bag overbalances and crashes to the floor, where it breaks open, sending a landslide of CD cases skittering across the pavement and into the road. The driver gives me a pitying look before accelerating on.

27th March

I'm not saying I had some peculiar dreams last night, but it's amazing how many large dogs you can fit in the back of a car.

Teemu and I are driven by Harri to Tampere, then we take the train to Helsinki and hurry over to the nearby radio station where I have an interview scheduled. It's a small studio and currently extremely crammed as there's not only me and the presenter in it but also Teemu and my three-man camera crew, as well as a cameraman from the radio channel filming for their internet broadcast.

After that I check into my hotel room, which has a smell to it that makes it not a very pleasant place to hang around. After half an hour doing my emails I walk down the hill into the centre to get some fresh air and look for something to eat. I end up in a cheap café in the shopping centre above the main Helsinki metro station where a Chinese guy who doesn't understand English (not sure I chose the right place to look for something vegetarian) eventually grills me a feta *panini*. Not particularly interesting, perhaps, but I did just manage to get Finland, China, England, Greece and Italy into one sentence.

Leafing though the local paper I notice that Jay Reatard is playing Helsinki tomorrow. Jay is a big Adverts fan and has covered 'We Who Wait.' We've never met, but a couple of months ago he contacted me to invite me to support him in the USA this summer. I hadn't realised he was currently touring in Europe so when I get back to the hotel I fire off a quick email asking what time he arrives tomorrow in case we could get the chance to meet up before I leave for my gig in Hämeenlinna.

The venue for tonight is called 'On The Rocks' and is *Rock* with a capital 'R'. All the usual *Rock* paraphernalia is there, and staff who seem to wish I wasn't. I'm playing as support to a covers band – they cover *Rock* – called 'Boiled Monkeys' and they are soundchecking when I walk in. I'm not too sure why I am playing on the same bill as them because I will never be as *Rock* as they are, and my audience and theirs will never meet. Actually, my audience probably won't meet me either as the sound guy insists my stage time is 10:30, whereas the blackboard outside says the place doesn't open until 11:00.

I ask Teemu to go out and alter the timings. Normally I'd be getting the chalk on my hands myself, but I don't want to deprive my young tour manager of a valuable learning experience. It turns out that I have to go outside briefly before soundcheck too: when I try to sing I find that my lips are so cracked from the cold that it's too painful to open my mouth properly so I dash round to a local shop to get some emergency lip salve.

One thing about these *Rock* guys, they know their sound: soundcheck goes well and is over in a couple of minutes. After that I sit around while the crew film all the kitsch stuff in the club – the blue fountains, the fluffy dice hanging off the drum kit, the blackjack table, the L.E.D. sign scrolling *Tonight…TV…Smith* and *Be…A…Celebrity!* They tell me that the management warned them not to film any of the audience at the gig unless they're prepared to get a written form from each person giving them permission. Funnily enough, when a professional film crew arrive from Finnish National Television to film something about the Boiled Monkeys, such concerns evaporate. Their interview takes place in the dressing room, which leaves me out in the concrete backstage corridor, unable to get to my guitar when I'm supposed to start. Just as I'm pondering what to do, a fan comes backstage with a big camera and ask if he can film the gig. So, tonight there will be more cameras than audience!

But in fact, thanks to the fact that most of my regular Helsinki crowd have turned up early, there's a good amount of people in by the time I start and the gig is fine. All the same, there's a telling moment when I say from the stage, 'I hope to see you in August back at the Semi Final Club,' and everybody cheers.

Teemu is looking tired behind the merch table, so I relieve him so he can go and get some sleep and spend a couple of hours manning it myself, chatting to people as they go past, signing stuff, and selling a good amount of CDs too. Most of my audience leaves pretty quickly as the Boiled Monkeys play, but there's a steady trickle of late night drinkers coming in for whom *Rock* cover versions are just the thing. I hear something interesting from my friends in the Helsinki crew as they prepare to leave: the venue only started charging entry at 11:00, so all my crowd got in for free. Result!

At 2:30 I'm standing outside with the film crew and Kalle's girlfriend Ella, who is taking still shots for the project. We feel like having a final drink somewhere, and Ella is suggesting a few likely places in the centre. I'm feeling sleep calling, and my only priority is that I don't have to walk in the other direction from my hotel so we end up in a fairly boring bar almost next to the venue. We settle around a table with some beers and chat for a while about how unfriendly the people at the club were.

'I hardly got a word out of the soundman all night,' I say. 'It sounded great on stage, so after the gig I specially went up to him to thank him and I still couldn't get a thank-you or even a smile out of him.'

'Finnish people are like that,' says Kalle, 'Very reserved. If you compliment them, they have to run away.'

We talk about what we should do tomorrow. As I have most of the day free, the idea comes up of a boat trip over to one of the islands where the crew can film me looking around an old castle.

On the way back to the hotel I realise that all I ate today was the breakfast mini-roll this morning and the multi-cultural sandwich this afternoon. Now everything is closed so my evening meal, at 3:30 in the morning, is a Snickers bar from the hotel reception.

Just before I turn in, I check emails and find a message from Jay saying he's flying in at midday, Holiday Inn room 313, let's meet up.

28th March

I open the curtains to find that the skies are a heavy grey and snow is swirling down, a stark contrast to the crisp air and bright blue skies since I arrived. Last breakfast finished an hour ago so I put on my warmest clothes and battle my way through the snowstorm to a café around the corner for a toasted sandwich and a coffee, which in my state of hunger and fatigue seems like the greatest breakfast I have ever eaten. Kalle sends a text saying we'll have to abandon the trip to the island because of the bad weather, and I text back to say I have an alternative plan: the 'TV meets Jay' sequence.

The film crew pick me up in their car and we go to meet Jay at the Holiday Inn, a short drive from the centre. As we pull up I can see curtains part on the third floor and a figure gesturing at me. I wave back and when we get into the reception area Jay is already down there. We shake hands.

'Hi, that was you waving up there, was it?' I ask.

'I wasn't waving,' he replies, 'I was flipping the finger.'

Not exactly Stanley and Livingstone, but we're going to get along. He shows me a photo on his phone he took of the message waiting for him on his television when he got into his room: *Welcome MR. RETARD!*

The six of us somehow cram into the car and drive back into the centre, Kalle and Rene trying to lean back far enough to film me and Jay chatting. 'God, TV, I have so ripped off some of your songs,' says Jay at one point. 'I totally stole New Church.'

'I hope you're getting this,' I say to Kalle. 'I'll be needing it for my lawyers.'

We emerge from the underground car park into the Helsinki World Trade Centre which obviously leads to more filming. Finally we find a reasonably quiet bar where we can get a drink and film the 'TV & Jay in the pub' sequence. I notice that Kalle is looking miserable and ask him what's wrong. He sighs, 'We were too close to get any decent footage in the car and it's really too dark to film in here…'

'Let's just have a drink and not worry about the filming,' I say. 'Afterwards we can go outside and walk around for a while, you can film us out there.'

It all goes quite well. We amble around in the snow, past an ice rink, Jay and I trying to chat casually as the camera crew keep pace. Johu holds the boom mic over our heads and everyone out on the streets stares at us thinking, *who are these guys?*

However, Jay, trainers might seem like a good idea in Memphis but are not recommended in Helsinki.

Time to get going so we return to the underground car park and squeeze back into the car, cameras rolling. Johu is listening back in headphones to some of what he has recorded and seems to be having a problem with the equipment. He looks over from the back seat and gestures towards the CD player. 'Can you just turn the Hawkwind down?'

Jay looks at me in mock horror. 'Did he just say, turn the Hawkwind *down?*'

Out of the car park and through the crowded main roads, Jay suddenly says to the cameras, 'Look at that! Get that!'

In a large cemetery off to one side of the road a small group of people dressed in black have gathered around a priest at the head of a grave. A funeral is taking place, snow falling heavily down on the solemn gathering as the coffin is lowered. I turn the Hawkwind back *up.*

The camera crew drop Jay off at the Holiday Inn – great hotel, bad location – and me at my hotel – great location, bad smell – and Teemu arrives ten minutes later to drive me to Hämeenlinna in a car he's borrowed from Nini's mother. As we leave the outskirts of Helsinki he says, 'I just had an idea. On the way we'll be driving past Riihimäki, where I was brought up, and it has the tallest flagpole in Finland.'

Bring it on. We take a short detour especially to see the flagpole in its full forty metre glory. There's even a car park. Teemu points out the sign in front and says, 'There used to be another town in Finland that tried to claim they had a flagpole taller than this one, so we put the sign up to say that *this* is the tallest. Now it's official.'

Back on the motorway, Teemu suddenly points to the vast snowfield off to the right, where the dark figure of a fox is trudging forward, staggering in the deep drifts. Hope it doesn't have vole fever.

We arrive at the venue, The Suisto club, to find the complete opposite of yesterday's *Rock* extravaganza. The room is small and atmospheric, and the soundman gives us a friendly welcome. The manager breaks off a meeting to say hello, and we're offered coffee and something to eat. Soon the film crew turns up, just in time to get footage of the lightning-quick soundcheck, then Teemu takes me up the road to my hotel. It turns out to be the nicest one yet so I relax in there for half an hour while Teemu goes to visit a favourite Aunt.

Tonight is the last gig of the tour and I'm supporting a well-known Finnish singer/ songwriter called Tuomari Nurmio so there's sure to be a good turnout. Eighty tickets have already been sold and it looks like this little venue will be full. I'm pretty aware that this is not my usual audience – some of them look even older than me! – so I warm up with a few slower songs until I feel them getting on my side then gradually get into the more high energy stuff. I'm offstage by eleven, satisfied with my performance, and the cameras trail me back to the dressing room, where Tuomari is suited up and getting ready to play. Not wanting to disturb him with the film crew I head out towards the venue again, then as soon as we are out of the room I turn around and go back in, closing the door behind me with a little wave to the cameras as I shut them out. It's just like Fernando Rey in 'The French Connection.' Oscar material, I'm telling you.

And now my tour is over and it's time to enjoy some red wine from the generous selection of drinks available in the backstage. Every now and then I make forays out to the venue, to check some of Tuomari's set and to make sure Teemu is alright at the merchandising stand. He'll be driving back to Helsinki tonight and I've told him to just let me know when he wants to leave so I can take over. In fact he stays until shortly after Tuomari finishes, then we say our goodbyes. It's been a good experience travelling with him and I'm sorry to see him go. Back in the dressing room I spend another hour with Tuomari and the film guys. Still only two in the morning, so I should get a decent sleep before the trip home.

Well, that was the plan. At 2:30 I get a text message from Teemu telling me that tonight the clocks go forward an hour, just in case I didn't know. I didn't know – and suddenly it's 3.30. I text back saying 'You are a great tour manager!' – and actually he is, because it's these little details that can make all the difference. He could have just thought, 'Oh, TV probably knows about that already,' and not bothered to let me know, and then I would have been an hour late at the bus station tomorrow, missed the only bus to Helsinki airport, missed my plane home, be stranded in Finland for another day, and have to pay a fortune for a new air ticket the day after.

It's still hard to get away though, and it's after four before the film crew have packed all their things together and gone back to their hotel, leaving me and Tuomori for a final drink. Even then, it's not that final, because he suggests taking the remaining bottle of red wine and drinking it in his hotel room. I hate to see a fellow musician drinking alone. It's six by the time I leave Tuomori's hotel and struggle the short distance up the road to mine, staggering like a field vole. The usual thing: the nicest hotel of the whole tour and all I do in it is spend a few hours unconscious.

29th March

I'm really not enthusiastic about the idea of waking up in time for breakfast but I have to leave the hotel soon after that anyway to catch my bus and provide the film crew with the necessary 'TV leaves Finland' sequence. As I don't want to look as tired as I feel, I'm going to need a coffee and some time under the shower before I'm ready for my close-up. Disturbingly, the breakfast room is in the hotel basement, in what seems to be a nightclub. There's a bar, low lighting, and a spinning satellite ball hanging from the ceiling. A giant plasma screen on the wall shows the morning church service and the volume is switched up to full so that the mournful, minor key hymns blare around the room. It's enough to put me off my mini-croissant.

Back in the room I check through the schedule that Teemu wrote out for me yesterday and see that my bus leaves twenty minutes earlier than I thought so suddenly I'm in a rush. I spend the final half hour on my computer attempting to check in for my flight online, a fiendishly complicated operation as Finnair require me to provide everything from favourite colour to shoe size.

I get down to Reception just as the crew arrives. I explain about my mix-up with the timings and tell them that if they want to get the shot of me leaving the hotel they'd better set it up now because I have to dash for the bus. 'One minute,' says Kalle, and they hurry out into the snow and set up their tripod and sound boom. I wait the one minute then hand in my room key and bustle outside, ignoring the crew. I speed down the road until I hear Kalle's voice behind me. 'Cut! TV, you are going the wrong way.'

'No, no, you can go this way – down here then left,' I bluff.

Idiot.

They trail me down to the bus station, a depressing 50's concrete construction that reminds me of every other bus station in the world. Airports are shiny, exciting places, even train stations have character, but bus stations always make you feel like a loser.

We sit around for the ten minutes before the bus arrives, take some souvenir photos of each other and chat about the tour and what a great time we've had. I feel friends with these guys now and sad to be leaving them. But we have to film the last sequence, the one where I get in the bus and go. And that means we have to say a quick goodbye now because they're going to have to set up the cameras outside and I'm going to have to walk straight past them as if they don't even exist. It doesn't seem right somehow – I want to be giving them all a big hug, even though it's not the Finnish way. Instead I have to think of my Oscar. I ignore them and get on the bus, then sit there in the back ignoring them still as they train their cameras on me through the window and the bus pulls away. Everyone else looks round at me wondering what's going on and I just pretend to be who I am.

Just a normal conversation...

apart from these guys

Advert for next volume of
tour diaries

You've never got a kairata
when you need one

Just a normal walk around
Helsinki...

and these guys

You have to admit it,
that's one tall flagpole

Bus stations are for losers

3. THE LAST DAYS OF JAY (2009)

PART ONE: SETTING UP THE U.S. TOUR

I've played tours in the US before and at the end of each one I leave the country unsure of whether I'll ever come back. Usually my friend and occasional tour agent Bryan organises the gigs and we've only had partial success so far: good turnouts in the larger cities but all too often empty clubs elsewhere. Fees have been so low that I've had to sneak in on a tourist visa and hope I get away without being noticed at Immigration. Now at last it seems like a worthwhile tour is on offer, but it's a long journey to make it happen…

15th July (2008)

Bryan has become aware of a musician called Jay Reatard who has recorded a cover of a song I wrote for The Adverts called 'We Who Wait.' He emails Jay's agency to suggest we play some dates together.

20th December (2008)

Five months after the July email, Bryan gets a reply from Jay Reatard's management and forwards it to me: *Jay is planning a US tour in June 2009 and wanted to invite TV Smith to join him as support. Would that be something he would be into?*

Yes it would.

12th January

After a few unanswered emails, Bryan finally hears back from Adam, the guy who's looking after Jay. They're intending to tour from June 11th to the 17th, gigs all along the West Coast including San Diego, Los Angeles, San Francisco, Portland, Seattle, and Vancouver. Great! Except that I have two UK gigs already booked in that period – Aylesbury on the 12th and Kingston on the 13th. Bryan and I speak on the phone and agree to provisionally say yes to the tour and see what develops. Apart from not wanting to let down the two UK venues, I have concerns about how to finance the trip – there's been no mention of a fee, but there will be flights and hotels to be paid for and also there's the sticky issue of whether I'll need a visa and how much that will cost. Bryan emails Adam, who tells him that at least I'll be able to travel in the van with Jay and band so I won't have any travel expenses once I'm over there.

22nd January

I've been offered two reasonably well-paid festival gigs in Germany right after the two UK dates. I could turn those down and still end up with the US tour not taking place – stranger things have happened. What to do? Bryan pushes Adam on the subject of fees and gets an assurance that I should get an average of around $250 a night. But put that against the flight and hotel costs and I'll probably still come out making a loss. And although I could still turn down the two gigs in Germany, the idea of cancelling the already-booked UK gigs bothers me. I float an idea to Bryan: *any chance Adam might be able to move the tour?* Bryan says he'll sound him out on it and also ask if there's any way to get a contribution towards the cost of the flight.

31st January

The first rough outline of the tour comes through by email. It's changed from West Coast to East Coast and it's got longer. More than two weeks of dates, shifted a week later so avoiding my UK dates. I don't want to miss this. The only question is, can I afford it? I'm all for sneaking into the country again as a tourist, but Bryan reckons because of the high profile nature of the tour and the fact we're going to have to cross the notoriously difficult US/Canada border, I'm going to have to get an official visa.

1st February

Bryan deals with a lot of bands coming over from the UK, and puts them through an agency to facilitate the visa application and make sure it gets through in time. The shock is, when all visa, union and agency fees are paid, the total cost is going to be in the region of two thousand dollars. This means there is now absolutely no chance I'll come out of this tour in profit. Is it really going to be worth it?

20th February

As well as playing a solo support set, Jay has suggested that I also play a few Adverts songs with him and his band. Despite the financial worries, it's time to stop sitting on the fence, so I give a final 'yes' to the tour. Bryan and I speak on the phone for two hours to discuss tactics and he says he will contact the agency so they can start proceedings to file a visa application for me. I learn that I have to prepare a thirty page press file going back to 1977 to prove that I am a 'culturally significant' artist.

10th March

Press kit submitted.

13th March

Visa application filed.

18th March

Adam sends over the tour as it stands, two weeks of dates, about half of them confirmed. The only one I'm not booked for is New York, where Jay plays on his own as part of a festival, but Bryan is confident he can get me a solo show on that day instead.

17th April

Dates for the tour officially announced. Starting in Chicago, heading up to Canada and back down the East Coast, ending up in Memphis. That all sounds good, but it means I need to get internal flights as well as the transatlantic ones and when I check the prices they are horribly expensive. Too late to turn back now.

23rd April

Adam informs us that a car company connected to the label Jay is on has agreed to pay for the flights. Result! I'm back on course to break even. We arrange that I'll fly from London to Chicago on the 25th of June, in time to meet Jay and the band for a rehearsal together before the first gig on the 26th, then at the end of the tour I'll get two flights – Memphis to Chicago, Chicago to London – to get me home.

13th May

Two months since the visa application was filed, the average time it takes to go through, but still no word back. I've been trying for the last few weeks to arrange sending some CDs to the US to sell on the tour but I'm getting nervous about it now in case the visa isn't approved. It would be a double disaster if I don't make it over but my merchandise does. A few ideas to help pay my way have already come up. Initially Jay suggested pressing up some vinyl copies of 'Red Sea' – he tells me his fans are hungry for vinyl and it would sell really well – but the label in the UK who own the recordings wouldn't let me. After some discussion, they agreed to let me have some CD copies at a reduced price instead. Also, a US label which released one of my recent solo albums has promised to send some copies to Bryan for me.

28th May

The guy at the US label's merchandising department makes an offer to manufacture cheap T-shirts for the tour, but I turn it down because I'm still worried about the possibility of the visa not being approved in time, or even if it is, having loads of shirts left unsold at the end. Bryan and I have a talk about what to do in New York, where I still need to find a solo gig. Most of the venues that I've played on previous visits – CBGBs, for example – have now closed down, so it looks like a choice between an intimate bar gig at Manitoba's or a venue called the Mercury Lounge where Bryan knows the booker.

29th May

Bryan says he's going to put on a gig by a reasonably well-known punk band at the Mercury and I could get on the bill too. We'll only be on a door deal, but it's the band's only appearance in New York, so we should pull a good crowd which will make it financially worthwhile.

30th May

I check the Mercury website and find that the other band is also playing there the night before. Bryan is furious and pulls the gig.

5th June

Full itinerary and fees for the tour arrive from Adam. Unfortunately only the first few dates are paying the full $250, most of the rest are only paying $150.

8th June

Bryan books me into the Mercury, in the middle slot between two bands I've never heard of. But it pays $200.

11th June

Still no sign of the visa. It's been three months since the application went in, and it's only supposed to take two. I email Bryan and he emails the agency, and we get a reply that they're hoping to get me into the embassy on the 22nd. Just a week before the tour starts…tight, very tight.

12th June

Today I'm playing the Aylesbury gig that initially clashed with the tour. After soundcheck I check into a B&B around the corner from the venue and am just unlocking the door to my room when I get a call from Bryan. 'Are you sitting down?' he asks. 'Your visa's been approved.' I'm in a pretty good mood for the gig, even though only forty people turn up.

15th June

The visa approval notice arrives at the London branch of the agency and they send me a copy of it by email, but I still need a final interview and digital fingerprinting at the American embassy before I can travel. We who wait.

17th June

CDs from the US label were sent to Bryan's place some time ago, but still haven't arrived. Even though the visa's been approved, we're struggling to get an appointment at the embassy for the interview. It could possibly have happened this week if there had been a cancellation, but the agency don't want to risk it as I have two gigs in Germany at the weekend and it's likely that after the interview the embassy will take away my passport to process it.

21st June

Back from Germany. Still no embassy appointment.

23rd June

One day to go before I'm supposed to fly out and still no appointment. I phone Bryan and he is as worried as I am. Half an hour later I get a phone call from the agency. 'Are you sitting down? You're not going to America…' There's a huge backlog at the embassy and they couldn't get me an appointment in time. Even the people working on the Harry Potter film can't get in. My first reaction is to abandon the whole thing. All that planning for this, I really don't feel like going on with it. Bryan says, think it over and get back to him in the morning.

24th June

I wake up feeling like fighting it. There must be a way to rescue the situation. Maybe, if I can just get an interview in the next couple of days, I could at least get there for the second half of the tour. The visa, if I ever get my hands on it, would last for three years, so it could be useful in the future, and next time I wouldn't have to go through this whole process, it would be sitting in my passport ready to go. The agency reckons they could get me in to the embassy within the week. If that works, I could fly to New York for the Mercury gig, then join the tour with Jay the next day in Brooklyn. Would mean paying for a new flight, full price. Not sure if I can do it.

25th June

Bryan tells me that the car company has agreed to pay for the new flight and the embassy has confirmed I will get an interview on June 30th. I could potentially fly out that night.

26th June

Curious about the generosity of the car company, I check out their website to see who I'm getting involved with. Their blurb says that their *long-term goal is to appeal to Generation Y consumers*. Hah! The agency calls to say they have a cancellation on June 29th so I can go in to the embassy a day early. They say I should be there at 7:00 in the morning to make sure I'm at the front of the queue. Passport could still take 48 hours to come back so Bryan arranges to book the flight for the evening of the 1st to give us two working days, just in case. Have to cancel the New York gig though.

29th June

I'm up at six and at the embassy just before seven. Third in the queue. There's a short interview, where the lady asks me which cities I'm playing in, and when I mention Nashville she says, 'Oh, do you play Country music then?' Well, not exactly but this is probably not a good time for the 'P---' word. I tell her I play 'singer songwriter kind of stuff.' Then I provide my digital fingerprints, she takes my passport, I pay twenty pounds to the courier company for their express delivery service to get it back to me as soon as the visa is attached and I'm out of there by nine. Lisa, the representative from the agency, tells me that she's 100% sure I'll get the passport back in time for my flight – even though the embassy says it could take from three to five days it's usually back in twenty-four hours and never takes more than two days. Bryan mails to say the CDs from the US label have just arrived. If I get there, at least I will have something to sell!

30th June

Five in the afternoon and the passport still hasn't arrived. I fly out at eight tomorrow evening and if I don't get it in the next twenty-four hours it really will be the end of my attempts to get on this tour. There are some panicky phone calls between me, Bryan, and the agency, and within the hour I hear back from Lisa that the passport has left the embassy and is on the way to her office. It could arrive any time between five past six and eight-thirty, she tells me, and she'll give me a call as soon as she has it. It's not until on the dot of eight-thirty that she rings back. 'The envelope's just arrived,' she says. 'I'm opening it now…' It's like the fucking Oscars. 'There we are, you are officially approved to work in America for three years.' She'll send it by courier to me tomorrow morning.

1st July

It's now nearly a year since Bryan's first email suggesting this tour. With just four hours to spare before I'm due to leave for the airport, the passport and visa arrive. I've missed Chicago, Detroit, Cleveland, and the two dates in Canada that I was particularly looking forward to and were the main reason I had to get a visa in the first place. The fees from those first five dates have now gone from the balance sheet, leaving only the lower-paid ones, and I won't arrive in New York until a couple of hours after my scheduled gig at the Mercury. But, Brooklyn, Boston, Philadelphia, Washington, Asheville (*where?*), Knoxville (*er?*), Nashville, Memphis, Oxford…here I come!

PART TWO: THE U.S. TOUR

Six hours time difference, and I get in to New York just before midnight. Bryan is at the airport to meet me. I didn't sleep a wink on the flight but I feel surprisingly good, happy to finally be here. Bryan drives us over to a seedy late bar in Brooklyn, a few blocks away from where he lives, and even though the music is too loud to allow conversation and the air conditioning is so brutal that my T-shirt is flapping in the gale, I feel like we are celebrating: we have pulled this tour back from disaster. A couple of beers, then Bryan drives me back to his apartment and shows me into the bedroom his two year old daughter Thalia usually sleeps in.

2nd July

I sleep a solid six hours but then am suddenly wide awake and up in time to say hello to Bryan's wife Alyssa as she heads off to record an interview to promote a book she's just published. Then over the next couple of hours I finish off the pot of coffee she's left and answer my emails. When Bryan wakes up we take Thalia with us for a short walk around the neighbourhood to pick up some food for breakfast. When we get back he sets up a microphone ready to record the links for a weekly radio show he's producing, presented by my old friend, fanzine writer and drummer Jack Rabid. Jack arrives around midday and tapes the introductions to the songs, then it's time to get over to a studio to record the next monthly special, which this month will be devoted to me. The plan is to record five or six songs live, then an interview about my past bands and solo career. Jack first saw me play in Harlow in 1989 when I was with Cheap, so we'll have plenty to talk about.

We are held up in traffic on the way to the studio, so even though I put down the five songs in one take, we're still running late for soundcheck by the time we finish the interview and have to hurry off to the venue. It's only a twenty minute drive away, but just as we arrive there's a sudden downpour which forces us to sit in the car for ten minutes, the rain hammering on the roof.

Eventually, increasingly worried about being late, we decide to dash through the rain into the venue, only to find Jay and band still soundchecking. I walk up to the high stage to say hello to Jay, drummer Billy and bass player Stephen, and shake hands with them all. *Hello, I'm TV. I am not always this wet!*

The band finish their soundcheck and I get up to run through the songs we're going to play together. We're all a bit nervous. First off, we have a go at 'Bored Teenagers.' The vocals come in right at the beginning of the song and it takes me a few seconds to realise that the band are playing it considerably faster than I usually do and I have to do some catching up. But then we're in sync, and that and the other three songs are fine. Now things are getting exciting – the tour is really starting and there's a good chance we will have five hundred people in the audience tonight.

The rain has stopped again, and I step outside so that Bryan can get the required photo of me in front of my name on the billboard above the entrance. When I get back upstairs Jay is in discussion with a journalist from the New York Times who is writing a feature on him and reckons that he will need five hours of interviews to get everything he needs. Jay is currently talking about a musician friend of his who had been diagnosed with cancer. Just before Jay went on stage yesterday, he got a call from the family to say that the guy wanted to hear his voice but would be too weak to say anything himself. Jay was wondering what on earth he could say, but just as the phone was passed over to him the guy died.

Downstairs the venue is filling out and a local support band is coming to the end of their set. Time for me to get out there. A funny thing happens when I hit the stage: the audience erupts with approval and enthusiastically applauds every song. Somehow I hadn't allowed myself to believe that would happen until now, and I come offstage elated. It feels like this trip has been worthwhile already and there's still the encore of Adverts songs at the end of Jay's set to come.

I carry my guitar up to the dressing room and Jay's lawyer wanders in, confiding to me that Jay is absolutely terrified of messing up the encore songs. But when the time comes it turns out there's nothing to worry about – they bring the house down.

After the show there are quite a lot of people hanging around the three dressing rooms. A couple who say they are friends of Jay's come into mine and tell me how much they enjoyed the set, and ask me if I bleached my jeans myself. I tell them I did, and before I know it, the girl is telling me that the latest trend in New York is to have your asshole bleached white. I don't even know her and I'm having a conversation about bleaching your asshole?

'Welcome to New York!' she says.

The hubbub dies down after a while and Chris, the guy from the car company who paid for my flight, says that now is the time to do the interview for his radio show. He gets Jay back over into my room and sits us on the couch in front of the microphone. We have a lengthy chat during which Chris continually tries to provoke us into being controversial. It feels a bit self-consciously 'edgy' but is presumably what the company wants for its target audience. Towards the end of the interview Chris says, so will you guys be recording something together? I look at Jay and he looks at me. We hadn't previously discussed the idea but now it's been said.

Time to load out. Jay and band are staying at a friend's apartment, I'll be going back with Bryan and meeting up with them tomorrow morning. On the way back to the apartment Bryan gets a text from Alyssa to tell him that Thalia is asleep on the living room floor and to be careful not to tread on her when we come in. When I stay with people on tour I generally try to be a good guest and not tread on their children.

3rd July

Bryan drops me off at the flat where the band are staying. I carry my guitar and bags out of his car and into the band minibus, then we say our goodbyes. So now the tour is really starting and we are on the road! For about half a mile until we stop for breakfast in a diner just north of Williamsburg.

But then we are on the road!

A few hours up the freeway we reach a funky suburb of Boston called Alston, where we load into a large bar called Harper's Ferry, space for about three hundred people in front of the stage. The manager reminds me that he was running a club in Providence when I played there with the Midnight Creeps a few years ago. He's friends with the Creeps and passes on singer Jenny's regrets that they're out on tour themselves at the moment and so can't come to tonight's gig. I already know this because she sent me a My Space message that read: 'WAAAAAAAAAAH!'

We carry in the gear, then go to the small upstairs dressing room, which smells of cat's piss. A security guy comes up to check everyone's I.D. to make sure we're all old enough to drink, and when he gets to me and sees that I am clearly much older than him he apologises: 'Just one of those stupid rules.'

Downstairs at the bar I'm surprised to see my friends Jon and Sophie who've flown up from Miami. Jon introduces me to his friend Dave, who tells me that he hasn't seen Jon for years but he's just the same as when they were in the air force together thirty years ago. 'Jon was always the one who didn't give a fuck, always had his hair too long, was always late for duty. We used to have a time together guarding the nuclear missiles.'

'You two were guarding nuclear missiles?'

'Yeah, me and Jon and a bunch of crazy people like us. We had to fool around and have fun, it was so boring. There wasn't anything to do, we just had to be there all night, the planes waiting on the runway loaded with bombs. It was a push button war. We used to have a game where we'd run out to the plane, touch one of the bombs and run back before the MPs noticed.'

I'm having a conversation with people who played *touch the nuclear bomb*.

Jon tells me a joke he suggests I could try when I head down for the concerts in the South: 'What do you call it when you get 32 Southerners in the audience? A full set of teeth.'

Actually, I might give that joke a miss.

I have another great gig, and afterwards watch Jay's set from the audience at the side of the stage. Quite a few people come up and congratulate me while I'm standing there, and one guy hands me a large glass of beer.

'Oh, a beer – just what I feel like right now, thanks!' I say.

Stony-faced, he replies, 'I work for the beer company, it's my job to give a beer to the musicians.'

Cheers!

After the show we head over the road to a fast food place. While we're in the queue Jay asks me what I'd think about the idea of using the day we have in Memphis to record something together. This idea definitely seems to be in the air now. I say, 'Sure, but what would we record?'

Jay says, 'I don't know, something fast I guess…'

Just then a woman interrupts. 'Say, I love your pants, they match your shirt! What are you doing in town?'

'Oh, nothing,' I mumble distractedly, not wanting to lose the thread of the conversation. She waits for more, and Jay explains we just played a gig over the road.

'Oh really!' says the woman, and turns back to me. 'What's the name of your band?'

I sigh. 'You would really never have heard of me.'

Finally she moves on, but now the conversation I was having with Jay has dried up. A few minutes later the woman passes us again on the way out. 'Good night!' she says to Jay, then turns to me. 'And good night to you to, despite your aloofness.'

We drive out to a motel on the outskirts of town and hang around in the lobby while Stephen, who does all the driving and tour managing, negotiates the room rates with the woman behind the reception desk. I notice that she keeps looking over at me, and finally I hear her say, 'I don't want to seem rude but, it's just that, if we use *his* I.D. you could get the senior citizen discount.'

'What year do you have to be born to get the senior citizen discount?' I ask, while everyone else cringes in embarrassment.

'1957,' she says.

I qualify by one year, so me and the band get a four dollar discount off our rooms. 'You guys owe me big time,' I tell them.

4th July

Yes, the fourth of July, 'The day we kicked you lot out,' they all laugh at me in the van.

Alarmed by reports of potentially horrendous holiday traffic in Philadelphia we have made an early start. Halfway there we pull into a rest stop and Jay wakes up in the back seat. 'Which of you guys shit in my mouth while I was asleep?'

When we arrive mid-afternoon the roads are still remarkably clear. I call my old friend Dave Thompson who lives nearby, hoping that we'll see each other tonight for the first time in years, but he's just been listening to the warnings on the radio of traffic chaos this evening and has decided not to risk coming to the gig. According to the radio, at 9:30 the biggest fireworks display on the East Coast will be starting, then there's another one on the waterfront at 10:00 – my scheduled stage time. It doesn't bode well for a good turnout.

But there's no one on the streets – and no one in the club – as we load the gear up the steep steps to the first floor venue, thankfully small enough that even fifty people would look like a decent crowd. Hanging around in the dressing room after soundcheck I read on the internet that someone in Coney Island has just set the new record for how many hot dogs can be eaten in ten minutes. He managed sixty-eight, while the hotly-tipped Japanese contender only managed sixty-four and a half. It's estimated that between the two of them they ate around 19,000 calories.

Nearly time to start, and not surprisingly there's still almost no one in the venue. Unable to take the brutal air conditioning in the dressing room any longer, Billy and I stand outside in the warm evening, listening to the sporadic bangs and crackles in the distance and watching the occasional rocket whoosh up over the roofs of the houses.

Billy sighs. 'I used to get really worked up when people didn't turn up to gigs… but then I thought, who gives a fuck?' He casts a world-weary glance upwards. 'People would rather stand around watching little explosions…'

He talks about what it was like growing up in Miami. It's a different and more dangerous way of life down there, he explains, with crime and drugs everywhere. He tells me about one incident that stuck in his mind: 'Some guy came to the house at 4:30 in the morning. He was rapping on the door and hollerin' and finally my father woke up and went down to open it, and there's this guy there asking for Billy, which happens to be my name. The guy is going, "Is Billy home? Where's Billy? I got some shit for Billy." My Dad says, "I think you got the wrong Billy. Billy is my four year old son."'

Some guys who came to the gigs the last couple of times I played in Philadelphia arrive and we stand around chatting for a while. It's a good feeling to know I have some friends here, and when I get on stage they crowd at the front, shout for requests and give up lots of applause at the end of the songs. A reasonable turnout in the end, and a surprisingly good gig.

Afterwards I'm winding down in the dressing room while the band pack away their stuff, and one of the guys cleaning the club pokes his head round the door and looks around.

'Say, you guys keep a clean green room.'

'Not too bad, huh?'

'Not too bad at all. I'm okay with that.' He smiles and walks out.

I really am quite getting to like American people.

5th July

My second visit to the Black Cat in Washington. The last time, when me and Attila The Stockbroker were on tour, about thirty people turned up and we were battling against the noise from a metal band playing in the venue's larger room upstairs. This time I'm playing to Jay's sold out crowd — the room is packed to the rafters and Jay had to fight to stop the gig being moved to the upstairs room. Better a full small room than a half-empty large one.

I watch Jay's set from a raised DJ booth to the side of the stage, away from the heaving crowd, standing next to Ian MacKaye's brother who has come, he says, to represent Ian 'in flesh and blood' as he's busy in a band meeting. At one point he breaks off our conversation and points out something in the crowd to the heavily tattooed girl doing security. A girl fight has broken out in front of the stage involving much pulling of hair, and she jumps in to separate the combatants.

Afterwards I stand outside the back of the venue, drinking a beer and chatting with a few people. Some guy turns up with a few small fireworks. They don't look very impressive, but he says that he's heard that if you stick them in a lemon they're amazing. It just so happens that there's a lemon on the floor, thrown out from the kitchen, so he rams four of the rockets down through the peel and lights the fuses. They fizz a little, the lemon spins round a couple of times, and that's it. We're all rather disappointed, yet relieved.

Tattoo girl shakes her head, disappears indoors, then comes back out with some more rockets. 'These have been around for a while, let's celebrate!' she says. She kicks aside the lemon. 'This should work better,' she says, drops the stick of a rocket into a coke can, lights the fuse and steps back.

One of the guys standing around says, 'Hmm, you know, I don't think it should be pointing that way…'

Right then the rocket launches off with a strangled squeal and shoots right past us, crashing into the wall behind.

'Wow, that was excellent *and* dangerous,' says the girl.

The next one arcs straight towards the security camera, hits it square on the lens, then explodes with a pop and showers the wall with sparks while general pandemonium breaks out below as we jump out of the way.

Never mind the 4th of July, *that* was a firework display.

6th July

Today's a day off. We aim to spend most of it on the road and get at least halfway down to tomorrow's gig in Asheville. However, nothing could be more boring than a whole day travelling, and last night outside the Black Cat someone told us that the scariest roller coaster he's ever been on, a giant old wooden one, lies on our route. It seems only right that we should have a go on it. We're in no particular hurry to leave though – the coaster is in an expensive amusement park called King's Dominion, and if we arrive after 4:30 in the afternoon we'll get cheap entry tickets. Around eleven I check out of the motel and carry my suitcase and guitar over to the van where Billy and Stephen are waiting. Stephen is saying to Billy:

'I was sitting over there by the lake this morning smoking a cigarette when all these ducks started swimming over towards me, then they got out of the water and started, like, running at me with their wings up."

Billy: 'Wow. Did they honk?'

'They sure did. They honked like crazy.'

'Were you scared?'

'Hell yeah!'

'Did you, like, *run away*?'

'*Hell yeah*!'

Jay arrives and suggests we go and get some food before we hit the road. He finds a Vietnamese restaurant on the GPS and we drive over to it. I'm not really in the mood for a full meal this early in the day, and vegetarian options are slim – one – but I order some green tea. While we're waiting to get served, Billy tells me that his girlfriend Margaret works at the ticket desk in a museum in Memphis. The other day this kid came up to the booth and asked for a cheeseburger. Margaret was trying to explain to him that it's a ticket desk and she doesn't serve food when the kid's grotesquely obese mother came up and apologised. 'Sorry, he's always doing this. Whenever he sees a counter and someone standing behind it he thinks he can order a cheeseburger.'

Maybe some education required right there.

We drive on down the tree-lined freeways of Virginia, and I kill some time leafing through a newspaper. Apparently not all the Independence Day festivities were Hot Dog eating contests and rockets in lemons. One headline says, *Celebration On July 4th Shows A Deadly Side*, and describes how four men were killed on a remote North Carolina island when the truckload of fireworks they were unloading onto a dock exploded. 'It sounded like 40 minutes of fireworks going off in four seconds,' said the dock master.

Another article describes how one woman sitting at an outdoor holiday party in Lauderdale was hit in the thigh by a stray bullet that police believe may have come from 'revellers' nearby.

Revellers? What kind of revels involve randomly firing off bullets around the neighbourhood?

And so we pull into the vast empty spaces of the King's Dominion car park shortly after 4:30, stumble out of the van and head for the entrance. We have to go back to the van so that Billy can change his shorts for long trousers when it's pointed out to him that his manhood is making frequent unscheduled appearances, something particularly inadvisable when children are around.

The first roller coaster is a stand-up one where you have a kind of saddle wedged up between your legs to keep you in place. Me and Stephen take the front pair of saddles, and Jay and Billy take the pair behind. We go up and over the first drop, then as we hit the second peak I hear Billy's voice roaring behind me, 'OW, MY BALLS! MY BALLS!'

And so it continues on every drop. The saddle was a little tight.

The next coaster is a more conventional wooden one – not the giant one yet though, we're warming up to that. Billy sits next to me and we crank up the first slope. Just as we go over the top he bellows, 'BUTTERFLYYYYYY!'

I sit next to him on the next one too, just to see what happens. This time he lets rip with, 'HOLY FOLDING MOSES!'

Time for the big one, the one we were warned about last night, the one that has drawn us here like moths to a flame. It's a long way up and I'm aware of Billy kind of twitching next to me. Over the top we go, and as we hurtle towards the earth, he bursts into the middle section of Bohemian Rhapsody. I even join in. *'LET ME GO, LET ME GO-O-O-OOOOOOOOO!'*

Somehow it seems to help.

On the way out of the ride we see some girls pointing at something on the ground. There's a skunk shuffling along towards the Go-Carts track. It's getting a bit too dark to take a photograph, but it does enable me to tick the box marked 'skunk' on my *animals-I've-never-seen-in-real-life* list.

A few more hours on the road, and then it's late evening and time to find a motel for the night. We end up in a place in the middle of nowhere surrounded by desolate strip malls where all the shops are closed so dinner is beer and potato chips from the gas station, back in my room. Stephen livens up his diet with a takeaway container of chocolate breakfast cereal flakes and a bottle of milk. He tells me that downstairs there's a waffle making machine, so at least breakfast will be exciting. I've never made my own waffle before but I have a feeling that in the morning sleep will be more important.

7th July

I meet the others at the van at twelve.

'So, did you guys get up to make your own waffles?' I ask.

Billy sighs: 'No. Another pipe dream.'

Instead, we're going to stop for something to eat at a place called Cracker Barrel, one of a chain of restaurants which litter the freeways across America and which the guys say I have to experience. It's a theme restaurant purporting to deliver *olde worlde* US charm, with a large shop attached. Unfortunately, *olde worlde* means pre-vegetarian. The only viable option on the menu seems to be the 'Vegetarian Platter,' but on reading the small print it turns out that most of the dishes that make up the platter are made the 'traditional way,' which means they contain meat broth. The food arrives for the rest and I eye up the side order that came with Jay's dish hungrily. 'Are those corn muffins?' I ask, reaching casually towards them.

'Uh uh, not vegetarian,' says Jay, swatting my hand away. Made with lard. He tells me that even the tomato ketchup in America isn't vegetarian. 'It's hidden here in the ingredients under *natural flavorings*. That's where they put the meat in.'

At the next mall I hurry round an enormous supermarket which has deli and food counters but I can't find anything vegetarian except olives. Luckily I'm rescued by the Italian restaurant further down the strip which provides a vegetarian sub, huge *and* tasteless. Back in the supermarket to buy some water I'm struck by the portion size issue: all the fizzy sugary drinks here come in gigantic containers, but you can only buy water in tiny bottles.

On we drive to this evening's gig. Asheville turns out to be a laid-back town in the hills, the kind of place where old hippies come to settle down. As we drive in I see a lot of craft shops and organic food stores but it hardly seems like the kind of town to host a punk rock concert. Worryingly, the venue is the largest of the tour so far, a giant room that could easily hold a thousand people, and only a handful of tickets have been sold in advance.

I get on stage half an hour after doors open. The sound is great, the lights are great – but there are only sixty people in. Thankfully, about half of them are clustered at the front against the security barriers and giving me a decent amount of applause after the songs. The rest are way off in the distance by the bar, mere specks.

After the show I hang around the merch table for an hour and sell one CD.

When the venue closes we get invited by the owner of a hookah bar back to his club and we spend some time there, immersed in the cloying smell of apple smoke and the irritating sound of bad rap music. But the drinks are free. One of the barmen is English and holds forth about '77 punk rock which, he says, he knows all about. Back in the day he met all the bands, he brags, but curiously when Stephen tells him who I am he gives me an irritated look and says he's never heard of the Adverts. Somehow I get the feeling that I am cramping his style, the only Englishman in Asheville, so I leave him to it and wander out into the peace of the courtyard, where a misty moon hangs overhead, bathing the mountains in eerie light.

On the way back to the motel, Stephen tells me that whenever I was out of earshot the barman kept telling everyone that it was a shame I didn't get on with him just because he is English.

'That's not why I didn't get on with him,' I say. 'I didn't get on with him because he is a wanker.'

8th July

We stop for breakfast at an organic supermarket and café, then head on higher into the Appalachians, where the clouds snag on the densely-wooded slopes like smoke drifting up from the trees. Indeed, this area is known as the Smoky Mountains. The rain comes down and the air is cool, no sign yet of the threatened Tennessee heat and humidity.

I get an SMS message from Jenny of the Midnight Creeps. The gig they were supposed to be playing tonight has been cancelled so they're going to drive some thirteen hours to see ours. The band they're on tour with will also be coming along. They're called M.O.T.O, and I know of them because Vom is always playing them down his basement bar. My favourite song of theirs is called, 'I Hate My Fucking Job' and the lyrics go, *I hate my fucking job*. That's all.

The gig was originally scheduled in a tiny dive bar, but the promoter became worried that too many people would turn up so he has moved it to a swish larger club further up the street. We soundcheck and then all wander into the pedestrianised town square to get something to eat. Jay, Billy and Stephen go to an all-you-can-eat – or, as it says on the menu 'all you care to eat' – sushi place, while I grab a takeaway tofu salad sandwich from an organic café on the opposite side of the square and sit on a bench to eat it. A string quartet have set up and are playing 'A Day In The Life.' The air is warm and sticky. Dusk is falling.

Back at the club the Creeps have arrived and are waiting at the outside bar for us. Jenny is going to sing 'Love Songs' with me in my set, so we go into the club to try it out, sitting on a couple of stools in a dark corridor behind the stage. Actually we could have tried it out on the stage as I counted three people in as we walked through. Maybe this gig shouldn't have been moved from the smaller club after all. The song sounds good though, so we're looking forward to performing it. If only there was an audience. We head back out into the yard again, away from the supercooled air-conditioning, loud rock classics music and wispy dry ice smoke to join the rest.

Shortly before stage time Billy comes out to tell me that the sushi was a bad idea: he has been shitting blood. 'And it smells like sushi too. That is weird.'

We get into a discussion about the worst toilets in the world and Billy says he just can't use the ones they have in some European countries that are just holes in the floor. 'However you try and squat, it's going to end up in your pants,' he complains.

Jenny drops down to the tarmac with one arm stretched out behind to support herself and does a back-arching demonstration of how to avoid this problem. 'You should try bein' a *girl* on tour.'

Quite a few people seem to be looking our way.

Soon it's time to start. The small crowd in the courtyard come into the icy interior fairly quickly once I start playing and huddle up in front of the stage, possibly for warmth. I get a good reaction even though it's a big room, and afterwards a lot of people pass by me at the merch table and thank me sincerely, say it was 'awesome' and ask for photos with me. But after an hour I've only sold one CD.

Possibly aware that the evening has not been a huge success, the people running the club now seem keen that we leave as soon as possible. As we hurriedly pack the gear into the van Jay tells me that he was a victim of the sushi too and projectile vomited seven times in the backstage toilet before going on stage. 'I was playing with seaweed on my face, man.'

Maybe an all-you-can-eat sushi bar in the middle of the Appalachian mountains is something to be avoided.

The band need to get some food after their earlier purge and we end up in a deserted supermarket the size of an aircraft hangar. The Creeps have booked the same motel as us, so when we get back there I head up to their room and drink a beer with them. I pass on the moonshine, distilled by a fan of theirs who Fed-Ex-ed four bottles of it to them for the start of the tour. Soon the conversation is increasing in volume and decreasing in logic and I slip away to my room to get a few hours sleep.

9th July

Not too far to travel today, and we arrive at today's cheapo motel – just outside Nashville, under the flight path and surrounded by freeways – with a few hours to spare before soundcheck. It's beautiful sunny weather and the promised Southern heat seems like it's finally arriving. I go up to my room, kick the cockroach out, wash out my dirty clothes in the sink and hang them out on the balcony rail so the whole car park is treated to a display of TV Smith stage shirts and underwear. I'm feeling a bone-deep tiredness weighing down on me and though I don't usually sleep during the day, the bed looks very attractive. Just as I'm thinking about slumping down on it I get a call from Bryan to say that the journalist from the New York Times would like to talk to me about Jay for the interview. By the time I've finished that and taken my washing in from the balcony it's time to leave for the venue.

Driving into town there's disappointingly no sign of the Nashville I'd expected: rhinestone cowboys on every corner and country'n'western streaming out of every bar. In fact it looks like every other big city we've visited on the tour: bland and corporate, faceless strip malls and run-down apartment buildings – off in the distance, as usual, a cluster of shiny high rise blocks that mark a city centre that, as usual, I will not get anywhere near before I leave for the next gig. The venue looks pretty good though, a medium-sized low-ceilinged club with a courtyard. When we unload the gear, however, a problem becomes apparent: the box of guitar pedals Jay uses is missing, seemingly overlooked in the rush of the load out last night. They are an intrinsic part of his sound, and without them it seems unlikely that tonight's gig will be able to go ahead. He and Stephen hurriedly head off in the van to see if they can find a music shop still open.

With no band left to soundcheck, the girl mixing the sound sets the stage up for me instead, then leaves on her bicycle to go and feed her dogs. I while away the time nibbling on a few snacks from the dressing room and it's only after I finish the spinach dip that I happen to read the ingredients and see I've just had a UMM as it contains gelatine. Obviously the carrageenan and locust bean gum and corn starch weren't enough to thicken it. And the only spinach involved comes right at the end of the lengthy list under 'seasoning.'

The van pulls up and Jay jumps out with a bulging bag from a music shop. 'Bought 'em all again,' he says as he sweeps past. Now he has to spend an hour or two inputting all the settings on the new pedals before going on stage.

A local band plays first, then by the time I start the club is reasonably full and my set goes down well. When it's time for Jay the place has filled even more and there is much dancing and moshing.

Good gig, but after an hour at the merch I've only sold one CD.

We pack the gear into the van. Jay wants to go with some friends to a party, and Stephen asks me if I want to go as well or get back to the motel. I would really like to go and get some sleep, but feel a bit bad about him having to take me all the way out there and then drive back later to pick up Jay.

'Don't worry about that, I'll take you,' says Stephen. 'I'm your bitch.'

There's nowhere open for food so it's another gas station dinner – in my case a bag of cashews. It's only when I've already handed over the money that I notice I picked up the wrong packet, and I say to the woman serving: 'Sorry, but I meant to get salted, not honey-roasted, can I change them?'

She looks at me blankly. 'Oh, ah don't know ennerthang 'bout nuts.'

'I just wondered if they were the same price. Can I go back and swap them?'

'Well, ah just work here, ah don't even eat ennya that kinda thang,' she says.

Honey roasted it is then. *Bon appetit!*

Back at the motel under the flight path, where the prostitutes roam the corridors, I do something I haven't done before on this trip to America: I switch on the television. It's awful. I switch it off again. I prefer the sound of the crack party in the next room.

10th July

Tonight's a home-town gig for the band: Memphis. As we drive in they ask me what I want to do while I'm here – the inevitable trip to Sun Studios? Graceland? Actually, I would like to see the Mississippi but there's not going to be a lot of time: the latest plan for a TV/Jay record is to record the songs we play together live tonight for an EP, so we'll need to be at the venue early to set up the recording.

By the time we drop off Jay at his house there's only a couple of hours left before soundcheck so we scrap the tourist plans. I'll be staying at Stephen's place for the next two nights and we drive over there next. He lives in a big old house with his girlfriend Megan, and a guy called Will who is in a band called the Magic Kids. Despite suffering from multiple sclerosis and having to move himself around in a metal support frame, Will is ambitiously trying to promote himself and some of his friends as a teen pop band. They have recently had some interest from a big label and Will is obsessively working on the computer, trying to finish off a song he wants to play them. It's taken quite a while so far and he has reached the maximum amount of tracks the software will allow.

Peering over his shoulder at the screen, Billy says, '150 tracks. Are you nearly done yet?'

'We have a mix of it which I think is pretty good. Some of the S's are a bit sibilant but we could probably do some work on the E.Q. to help that.'

'I guess no one's going to mind too much,' says Billy. 'People aren't going to be saying, *I HATE that song. The S's are waaay too sibilant!*'

Off to the venue, a fine slice of Americana called the Hi-Tone Café which at one time used to be Elvis's dojo. Among the memorabilia plastered over the walls is a photo of him in his karate robes, kneeling next to his instructor in this very room.

Soundcheck takes longer than usual as we need to get everything right for the recording. When it's all sorted out the band hang around chatting to their friends, and I sit on the steps outside for a while, watching the traffic and enjoying the evening sunshine.

Memphis doesn't let me down and the gig is a triumph. It's just slightly disappointing that we kind of mess up the songs we play together which will probably scupper the idea of releasing a recording of it. Never mind, the gig's the thing. I stand behind the merch stand when the show finishes, and get told a number of times that I am 'awesome.' It's a word I've heard often over the last week, and tonight it even translates into sales: two CDs!

Most of the band's friends end up in the dressing room – and they have a lot of friends. Over the constant roar of the giants fans wafting the oppressive air around, many shouted conversations take place all at once. One woman asks me, 'Have you had time to try a real Memphis barbecue since you've been here?'

'Well, no – and I'm a vegetarian so I guess there wouldn't be that much I could eat?' I reply.

She takes a step back. 'Ah, a vegetarian! Nooo, you don't want to be getting involved in the Memphis barbecue.'

The soundman comes in and tells me, 'I am so full of meat. The last three days I have eaten nothing but meat. Today I bought this big hunk of meat and while I was waiting for it to cook I started eating these other slices of meat, and then when the meat was ready I wasn't really hungry any more but I didn't want to waste it so I ate that too. I am full of meat.'

He may be telling this to the wrong person.

Eventually the party ends up at Jay's house. It looks like things could go on here for some time – there's talk of getting in the pool – but Stephen and I are both exhausted so after a quick drink we tell Jay we'll phone tomorrow morning to sort out what time to leave for the final gig of the tour in Oxford, then we head back to Stephen's place.

Kill the cockroach. Go to sleep.

11th July

Jay's phone isn't switched on, must have been a good night. Stephen suggests that while we're waiting to hear from him we drive to the store and pick up some food for breakfast and for when we get back from Oxford tonight. He also needs to get a gift for his niece – it's her birthday today and he has to drop in to her party before we leave for the gig.

Stephen has a big old sedan car parked around the side of the house, so we climb into that and pull out onto the road. The speedometer doesn't work, but he explains that a new one costs 600 bucks whereas a speeding ticket only cost 40 bucks so he can get quite a few tickets and it will still be a lot cheaper. The air conditioning doesn't work either, but the windows open.

We split up and I roam around the store for a while, picking up some salads and other healthy stuff my body is craving, and when we meet back at the exit Stephen is carrying a child-sized helium balloon of a character called Dora The Explorer which bobs over his head on a piece of string. We stuff her into the backseat with the groceries and she floats around back there on the drive back. What with the wind streaming in through the open front windows she becomes quite agitated, and occasionally tries to get up front with me and Stephen. She is attracting quite a few looks from the guys riding in the back of the pick-up truck in front of us.

We leave Dora in the car while we unload the groceries, then discuss what I want to do while Stephen is at the party. Jay's offer to take me out to see a few sights is not going to happen because he's still not answering his phone. Stephen says he could drop me off at the Mississippi but getting back afterwards would be complicated. Or there's the possibility of going for a walk?

'Hmm,' says Stephen, pointing off to the right, 'the neighbourhood is alright for a few blocks this way but looks pretty much just like this.' He moves his arm round ninety degrees. 'This way is dangerous. Uh, *this* way is dangerous and *this* way is dangerous.'

On the other hand, staying in and eating that vegetarian tamale I just bought seems an attractive option.

Stephen goes off to his niece's party and arrives back an hour later. He tells me that the parents had hired someone in a big green Elmo costume to entertain the kids. First of all he was happily dancing with them, then one girl suddenly got scared and all the rest of the kids panicked too. 'I have never seen so many terrified two-year olds in one place,' Stephen says.

But Dora had a good time and decided to stay.

Still no word from Jay, and after ringing around a few people, Stephen finally gets hold of someone who was round at Jay's last night and hears that the reason we can't reach him is that after we left he jumped into the pool with his phone still in his pocket.

So we head off in the van, first picking up Billy and Margaret, then over to Jay's place to pick up him and his girlfriend Lindsay. Then it's back to last night's venue to load up the gear, a quick stop on the outskirts of town at an authentically shabby Mexican diner on the edge of a trailer park where they have nothing whatever vegetarian – except the bottled water – then finally we hit the road for Oxford.

The GPS takes us down a parallel road to the highway, bumpy and narrow, the vegetation all around strangled by Japanese kudzu weed, imported in the fifties to control soil erosion and now running out of control so that the landscape has a surreal amorphous appearance, with here and there the bare grey tips of dead trees poking through the rolling green blanket of vines. Jay explains that it was originally used to make vegetarian jelly, as an alternative to gelatine.

'Is there any way to get rid of it?' asks Lindsay.

'Maybe if vegetarians eat more jelly?' I suggest.

Eventually we reach a 'Road Closed' sign and the route ahead peters off into a dirt track. Jay's voice comes over from the back seat, 'Right now Tim's thinking, this is where we kill him and steal all his money...'

The venue turns out to be a pizza restaurant, and they don't seem that thrilled to see us turn up while they still have plenty of diners at the tables. We load the gear in and dump it on the stage. There's clearly going to be no soundcheck, and Stephen and Jay have to go to a meeting with one of the record labels they're involved in so the rest of us have some time to kill. The air conditioning in the restaurant is so fierce that I can't sit in there for long, but backstage is the opposite end of the spectrum – a basement at the back of some storage rooms smelling strongly of black mould. You can only get into it by walking down the hill at the side of the restaurant and pushing a door that looks like it leads nowhere.

I take a walk around Oxford in the sultry evening air, but it's basically one small town square that looks like a stage set, the shops – mainly selling upmarket tat (a divan for your dog, anyone?) – all closed.

Backstage the support band are sitting around in some old sofas, there's a large crate of beer on ice, and some enormous bowls of taco chips. I steer clear of the spinach dip. At least I know my haul from the supermarket will be waiting for me later when I get back to Stephen's. Meanwhile the evening is dragging and this is not a nice place to be. At one point I hear Lindsay's voice in the distance, sounding a bit nervous: 'Hello? Helloooooo?!' Her head appears around the door. 'Oh thank God, I was getting kinda scared there.'

Worryingly, it's only half an hour before the support band are supposed to start, and when I last went up the road to see what was going on in the club I counted five people in the room.

Jay and Stephen get back from their meeting and the first band head up the road to play to no one. Then it's me, playing to about thirty reasonably enthusiastic people, and finally Jay crowning the evening with about seventy in. What a weird way to end the tour. Missouri has strict alcohol laws, and at the stroke of twelve the lights go on and anyone with any remaining beer in front of them has it taken away. I'm standing behind the merch table and even mine gets taken away.

Back down to the depressing backstage room where we can drink in peace, and this is where I find out there has been a change of plan: instead of driving back to Memphis tonight, Jay has decided we're all going to stay here in Oxford. He's going to get a room so we can party all night!

Slightly annoyed because all my things are back at Stephen's place, not to mention that good food, I say, 'Make that two rooms.' They might want to party all night but I have a long flight back to the UK tomorrow and will need to get some sleep at some point.

We finish off the drinks in the backstage, then suddenly Jay seems in a rush to leave. Just as I'm climbing in the van, Billy – still standing on the pavement – says, 'Well, I guess this is goodbye.' He and Margaret are driving back tonight. This catches me by surprise – ten days on the road together and suddenly he's gone.

Hoping to crash the end of tour party, a couple of other friends of Jay's take Billy and Margaret's place in the van and we set off. Finding a motel isn't as easy as we hoped. We follow the directions on the GPS, but the first two places we try have no rooms free. The third is absurdly expensive. There's some unrest in the back of the van as Jay and Stephen head out for the fourth attempt, in a motel with an improbably palatial lobby, a massive glittering gold chandelier filling the cavernous space above the front desk.

While the guys are in the lobby talking to the manager, I stay in the van with the girls, who like me would very much like to find out where we're going to stay. We are watching the lobby like hawks, trying to read the body language between the receptionist and Jay to see if this place is going to let us in.

'Look, look! He's reaching for his wallet!' I say. 'That's got to be a good sign!'

'Is it always like this?' asks Lindsay with a sigh.

'Often,' I answer. 'You have to be flexible otherwise it's impossible to bear.'

And in fact, even though I am separated from all my worldly possessions and don't know yet where I'm sleeping tonight, against all the odds I actually am having a good time. You have to make the most of it because if you don't enjoy getting there you won't enjoy being there.

Eventually we're in. I drop my guitar off into my room and then head back around the quadrant to the other room, where the party is in full swing. I'm there for some time, I couldn't tell you how long. There is talk, laughter. Jay is telling me we should make an album together: he'll write the music, I'll write the lyrics, he knows a label who'll put it out. After some time I leave the rest to it and float back to my room in the warm misty rain.

My own room! Privacy! I even have my emergency toothbrush in my pocket, almost as if some second sense told me I would get separated from my bags tonight. However, I give up on brushing my teeth when I can only get hot water out of the taps.

12th July

I thought I had it bad not being able to clean my teeth. In the party room, they tell me, they had to drink vodka and hot water.

We're all suffering a little from last night, and food is required before the trip back to Memphis. We eat in the 'Old Venice Pizza Restaurant' – although I don't think old Venice would have approved of a pizza that seems to have been cooked in a microwave.

Then it's time to leave – I have my bags to pick up and a plane to catch. We judder our way down the freeway, and Stephen voices all our feelings when he says from the driver's seat, 'Dude, the road between Oxford and Memphis is the bumpiest road in the country.'

Everyone's feeling queasy after an hour and I suggest that before I leave for the airport we could do some bonding with a group vomit. On the way into the city that almost becomes a reality when we pass a church entirely painted a stomach-churning purple, right down to the railings around it. 'I believe Al Green preaches in there,' says Jay.

Well, I didn't see Graceland and I didn't see Sun Studios and I didn't see the Mississippi, but I did see Al Green's purple church.

I wave goodbye to Jay and Lindsay at their house, then Stephen takes me on to his place where I gather my things together and pack my bag in a panic, aware of my flight time nearing. Stephen finds a cap with a plastic propeller on the top and we take turns to wear it for the goodbye photos, then he drives me to the airport.

While I'm waiting to board, an announcement comes over the public address system warning that Homeland Security has just raised 'The Threat Level' to red. Just another airport announcement to keep us on our toes. There's something about that voice, though… that dusky drawl…those slurred Southern vowels. It couldn't be…

Or could it?

Elvis?

Footnote:
Almost exactly six months later, at the age of 29, Jay went to join Elvis. R.I.P Jay.

Punks in the park

Because it has to be done

Goin' up

HOLY FOLDING MOSES!

Goodbye from the
Addams Family

4. HAPPY BIRTHDAY TO YOU. AND YOU (2009)

<u>26th August</u>

A trip to Finland to celebrate two birthdays – my friends Jukka and Tommi both turn fifty this week and I'm coming over to play at their parties, which are being held in the clubs in Helsinki and Tampere where I would normally play anyway. Tour agent Harri has booked in a couple of regular gigs before the birthday gigs to help pay for flights and hotels.

The first gig is in Joensuu, many miles to the North-East of Helsinki near the Russian border and they want me on stage at seven in the evening, which means I have to leave home at five in the morning to get the earliest flight out of London. Even then I won't arrive at the venue until forty minutes after I'm supposed to start but there is no other way.

It's a two and a half hour flight to Helsinki, then a bus into the town centre, where I meet up with Tommi in the station café. He hands me over the train tickets for the next few days and we chat while I wait for my train. He tells me that his band UJO will be playing a few songs from their Abba Swedish-language cover versions set at Jukka's pre-gig birthday party on Saturday. I'm happy to hear that at Jukka's special request original Helsinki crew member Hessu will be appearing with them. They had a falling-out a while back which led to Hessu leaving the band and I've missed him.

Then I have a four and a half hour train journey to Joensuu. Antti, the promoter for tonight's gig, picks me up at the station and as we load my bags and guitar in his car he explains that I'll need to finish playing promptly at ten, after which there will be two hours of short films shown on a screen behind the stage, quiet enough not to disturb the neighbours who live upstairs.

We get to the venue just before eight. It's small, and comfortably full with the thirty or so people in there sitting at tables. When I walk over to the stage they all cheer, which is very heartening. It takes thirty seconds to soundcheck, then I play for nearly two hours to a warm response.

The place gradually empties while the films play and soon after midnight there's just me and the staff left. I sit with Antti for a final beer, and he says, 'Great gig, and not a bad turnout for a Wednesday. Also, good considering tomorrow is the annual town holiday and they have free music on in all the bars in town,'

'The town has its festival on a Thursday?'

'Yes, they used to have it on a Friday but people were, well, *enjoying themselves* a bit too much so they moved it to Thursday.'

Careful, Joensuu. Don't enjoy your festival too much tomorrow or next year they might move it to Monday.

27th August

I hurry up the road to the station, where the stopping train to Pieksämäki is waiting. At least, I hope it's the stopping train to Pieksämäki — there are no destination boards on the platform and the waiting room is closed for renovation. I'm encouraged by the fact that the only other person in my carriage, a Finnish guy, asks *me* if it's the train to Pieksämäki — surely we can't both have guessed wrong.

I'm still relieved when we pull into Pieksämäki right on time a little after two hours later, and from there I change on to an Inter-City train for another hour into Kuopio. Last night I was told that Joensuu and Kuopio are actually only 130 kilometres apart and the bus does it in an hour and a half, but I already had my train tickets.

It's a ten minute walk to my hotel. In the lobby, while I wait for the lift to take me up to my fourth floor room, I scan the listings on the poster for the club I'm playing at tonight, but my gig isn't included. My room overlooks the town square, where some kind of festival is in the process of packing away, although the empty stalls and attractions are being left in place, presumably to re-open tomorrow. Kuopio is bigger than Joensuu so apparently merits a two-day festival. Probably it used to be at the weekend but people enjoyed it too much.

Somewhere over the other side of the square lies the venue, Harry's Pub, just a few minutes walk away. That's handy, because when I go there for soundcheck at the agreed time of 5:30 there is no one in the venue so I have to go back to my hotel room. Once there I look up my contract. There it is: load in 5:00, soundcheck 5:30, dinner in nearby restaurant after soundcheck, onstage 10:00 SHARP!! And a local support band playing after me at 11:00. Hmm, a short set and a band playing *after* me: a sure sign that the promoter thinks the audience will need some livening up after the boring solo act. Finally I find what I need — there's a phone number for the venue manager and for the technical person, Kimmo. I send Kimmo a text message: What time is soundcheck?

No reply.

At seven-thirty I go back to the venue. The door is still locked. I knock tentatively, then a little louder and draw a few looks from the group of people smoking outside the restaurant next door. I feel pretty foolish standing there with my guitar, next to a poster of myself with a guitar, clearly unable to get into my own gig, and slink away back to the hotel.

At eight I'm back. Aha, the venue is still shut but the bar next door is open! But when I go in there they tell me they are nothing to do with Harry's Pub, which opens at nine.

Back to the hotel. At five to nine I arrive back and still the place is shut, so I wander down the road and sit on a park bench for ten minutes. When I return, Harry's Pub is miraculously open! I go down into the cellar to find a stage already set up with a microphone, drum kit and amps, obviously all prepared for the support band. There is one guy in the room, and when I ask him about soundcheck he tells me that the soundman just left and will be back in half and hour. Fifteen minutes before I'm supposed to play. I explain that I've been trying to get in for the last four hours, but he just shrugs and shows me into the backstage dressing room. I sit there for a while, my eyes drawn inevitably to the graffiti-covered walls, puerile obscene drawings and posters for rock and metal bands. No sign of any punk.

Out in the club the music has started up from the DJ booth. It is, as I feared, Rock with a capital R. I get the distinct feeling that this is not a suitable venue for me. As the guitar solo on 'Freebird' winds it weary way towards the end, the guitarist from the support band arrives and introduces himself. Fearing the worst, I ask him what kind of music his band plays and unexpectedly he tells me that they are a punk band, doing some covers and a few songs of their own. 'Actually, we are kind of surprised to be playing after you,' he says.

So am I.

The soundman turns up. 'Are you Kimmo?' I ask.

'No, he is in Helsinki. I was asked to stand in a couple of weeks ago.'

That would explain why Kimmo didn't reply to my text message. I ask if the manager is around.

'No, he is on holiday in South America.'

Good job I didn't text him too.

Still not many people in the venue, maybe around forty, but I have to get onstage at 10:00 SHARP! It's a relief to find that the soundman knows his stuff and after just a few words into the microphone and some tentative strums on the guitar everything sounds great. I get straight into it and the audience are with me from the first song, the applause getting louder and louder as more people drift in and stay. I stretch the set to the absolute limit of eleven o'clock, and then there is such a demand for an encore that I play a couple more songs. When I go back into the dressing room the other band seem kind of shocked that they have to go on after me.

I slip out into the venue and set up my merchandising on a table near the stage. People cluster round and tell me how much they enjoyed the gig. One girl says, 'It was amazing how much energy you put into that. You are exactly the same age as my dad. The most energy he ever spends is chopping wood.'

Mind you, chopping wood is hard work.

The other band start off and are actually quite charming. And they surprise me with a good punky cover of Billy Bragg's 'New England.'

Backstage we sit with a few beers and a bottle of Finnish Jaloviina brandy, everyone much more relaxed now the gig is over. The girl bass player points at the star on the neck of the Jaloviina. 'This is the lowest grade,' she says. 'There is also a three star version, but this is the one musicians prefer.'

'Yes, there's a one star Jaloviina and a three star Jaloviina,' says the guitarist, 'but the strange thing is there is no two star Jaloviina.'

'Maybe the Swedes have it?' says the girl.

The guitarist points to the label on my Karhu beer. 'And do you know what this "III" means under the word Karhu?'

'Does it mean you can drink three before you fall over?'

'No, it was actually a sign of how much the beer used to be taxed, according to its strength. There was a "I" and a "III" and even a "IV" – that one was really strong.'

'But no "II"?'

He thinks for a moment. 'That's right, no "II".'

'Probably the Swedes have it,' says the girl.

The Jaloviina goes round.

It's impossible to sit there and ignore the graffiti on the walls, much of it comprising sketches of male genitalia in a state of arousal. 'Maybe,' says the girl thoughtfully, 'I should draw a huge cunt.'

'What is it about musicians?' I say. 'Every backstage room I've been in is like this.' I point out one prime example: "If you want to see a bad drawing of a guy fucking a horse, this is the place to be. Oh, and there's one of a man fucking a dog.'

The drummer chimes in. 'There's one up there of a man fucking a woman!'

How weird.

Among the selection of drawings there are also a lot of band names. The drummer points out the name of one musician with some more writing scrawled underneath it. He translates: *Manly and thin. BOTH AT THE SAME TIME.*

'Actually,' he says, 'this guy is fairly well-known here – he's the great great grandson of Sibelius, the Finnish composer.'

'Was Sibelius thin?'

'No, he was a fat bastard.'

Well, it's time for me to go back to the hotel.

28th August

I had a dream that I could talk to the animals. When I wake up and look out of my window, a large inflatable giraffe is looking in, and the festivities in the town square are in full swing.

A decent hotel breakfast, then I hurry up the road to the station, another four and a half hour train journey ahead of me. In Helsinki, the hotel Tommi has booked – a good one too – is literally across the road from the station, and I have a half hour in there before wandering up the road to soundcheck at the Semifinal, one of my favourite clubs in Europe. The location isn't quite as good as it used to be though – when I first came here it stood at the top of a slope with a panoramic view across the bus and train stations and the rest of the city. The club hasn't moved but an enormous modern shopping centre has been built where the bus station used to be and the only view now is of towering glass-fronted buildings. Standing outside the club with Tommi after soundcheck, waiting for his wife Annastina to arrive with the birthday cake, he tells me sadly how he and the Helsinki crew used to rehearse in the same building as the Semifinal when they were teenagers, and at the end of the night they'd race for the last bus home, rolling drunkenly down the snowy slope and arriving at the door of the bus seconds before it closed. No chance of that any more – teenage years have gone, and the landscape that accompanied them. Nothing like a birthday to get you feeling all nostalgic and maudlin.

The official opening time for the club is ten, but Tommi has let his friends know that they can get in for free from nine for the official birthday celebrations. There's cake for all and a slideshow with lots of photos of Tommi and his friends through the years. One of them is of me, taken on stage in Germany years ago, the first time that Tommi and the rest of the Helsinki crew saw me play. Jukka, standing next to me, points out that this photo was where it all started: after that gig, Tommi and friends came home and asked him to try and set up some gigs for me. He talked to tour agent Harri, some gigs were arranged with Punk Lurex OK, then came the record with them and all the succeeding tours. Not to forget the stranger stuff – the gig up in the Arctic Circle in Rovaniemi where I met Santa, the lakeside festival in the forest a few years ago... Jukka confides to me now that he really only suggested most of those things for a joke and was a bit startled when I said yes because that meant he had to figure out how to actually organise them. And the latest thing he didn't really expect me to agree to was the idea of coming over for these two birthday parties.

Tiina from Punk Lurex OK arrives. Just recently she has tried to reform the band, but Riitta – who lives in faraway Seinäjoke – couldn't face the idea of the long journeys to rehearsal and anyway was tiring of being in a band so didn't want to rejoin. They played their first gig with a new guitarist and drummer just recently at the Puntala Rock festival, where I played with the original line-up a few years ago.

'How did it go?' I ask.

'Welllll...not perfect. The guitarist broke his arm so a couple of stand-ins had to learn some songs just before the gig and come on stage with us. The audience didn't think having three guitarists on stage was all that 'punk.' Then after the gig the drummer left.'

The place is already quite full for the birthday hour and by the time the paying guests have come in it's completely packed. The support band are an old Finnish punk band who Tommi has asked to reform for the evening. By the time they finish it's already past my scheduled 11:30 start time and I'm itching to get going. In the sweaty, crowded, close-up Semifinal I play one of the best gigs I can remember, and manage to include quite a few songs from 'Cast Of Thousands', which I know is one of Tommi's favourite albums. Even as I walk off stage I know there are going to be quite a few encores, but someone standing at the side of the stage is trying to get my attention. I'm torn between the applause from out front and this one person earnestly gesturing at me.

'TV, I know you are busy, I just want to tell you something.'

This sounds important. For a moment I let the noise of the room slip away and I listen to what he wants to say. He leans in.

'Thank you. You made me remember who I am.'

And then it's back on stage.

29th August

Tommi meets me at the station. He and Annastina are taking the same train to Tampere so they can go to a football match there with Jukka in the afternoon. On board, we head straight for the buffet car. Tommi needs a beer, he says, because he looked in the mirror this morning and his eyes were 'glassy.' Settled down at a table, he tells me that for a short while in the 80's he had a band covering exclusively Adverts and Explorers songs, and he called it RexProles d'Artsev. While I was in England bemoaning the fact my first two bands had broken up and I was a failure I had no idea I was being anagrammed in Finland.

At Tampere I leave Tommi and Annastina to their football match and head to the hotel Jukka has booked for me – a good one too – literally across the road from the Telakka, where I will be playing this evening. *Note to self: must play more birthday parties, you get better hotels.*

At five I go to the venue. Soundcheck takes thirty seconds, then I go upstairs for another soundcheck in the room where the pre-gig birthday party event will take place. Champagne is being poured by the bar staff and slowly the guests trickle in until the room is fairly full. Every guest is given a small pamphlet with some of Jukka's photos, stories, and lists of his favourite records – including quite a few of mine – in it. On the front, underneath a cute photo of him as a baby, are the words 'From this…', and on the back, '…to this', over a recent photo of him looking drunk, pulling a silly face and wearing a gold cardboard party crown crookedly on his head.

I have a quick word with Harri, who is seated with his wife at one of the tables. They are tired and rather sad: today they got up at 3:00 a.m. to take their daughter to the airport. She was flying out to Canada to start her university studies there, and tonight they will go back to an empty home.

Then Jukka says some words – quite a few words, actually – to the assembled guests, speaking without notes and eliciting many chuckles from his audience. After this the buffet is started, and I slip into the dressing room to avoid the temptation to eat – it's much too near stage time to risk it now. After the guests have had coffee and cake, Jukka introduces me and explains how we first met, then I play the three songs he has requested. I'm followed by a German singer/songwriter called Marti who I met previously when he put on a gig for me and Garden Gang in a small town near Nuremberg and then again when he came to Jukka's lakeside festival in the forest. After that UJO perform and are as hilarious as ever as they go through their Abba routine, clumsily attempting all the dance movements with a heart-warming enthusiasm, so ridiculous that it becomes high art. Instead of the T-shirts of Abba members they usually wear, this time they are wearing T-shirts bearing a photo of Jukka as a teenager.

I sit next to Tiina watching them, and we both agree how great it is to see Hessu back with the old crew. Outside some fireworks explode in the distance. 'That's at the Särkäniemi amusement park,' says Tiina. 'My son is there with his father.'

'How old is he now?' I ask. Last time I saw him he was a toddler.

'Twelve,' says Tiina.

Twelve? I guess we won't be watching Asterix cartoons together on TV again.

'Why are they having fireworks?' I ask.

'It's the last day before they shut for the Winter.'

But it's still August, I'm thinking. Then I realise – here in the far North, Summer is already almost over.

As the upstairs party breaks up to prepare for the downstairs gig, Jukka thanks me for the performance and says, 'Looking at you I know there *is* life after fifty. Well, at least three years.'

Downstairs the room is packed and my gig goes well. I play for nearly two hours then sit on the stage selling the few CDs I have left. A lot of people ask for hugs and leave with a lot of my sweat on their clothes. One girl says, 'I am thirty years younger than you. Now I *see* what I want to be in thirty years.'

There's an hour left to drink and chat with the rest of my friends before the Telakka closes, then there are a lot of goodbyes. I feel another wave of nostalgia wash over me. Already a tour is being planned for next February, but I won't see any of these lovely people again until then.

Outside I have a chat with Hessu. 'Still warm for this time of year,' he says, although I can feel a chill in the air, the unmistakeable taste of Autumn approaching. As he prepares to leave I am thinking – but don't say – why can't the Helsinki crew just make up and be best friends again? Come to that, why doesn't Tiina get the original Punk Lurex back together – invite Sami back on drums and persuade Riitta to come back from Seinäjoke. Why can't everything be just like it used to be?

Bloody birthdays.

5. CONCRETE JUNGLE (2009)

23rd September

Yellow fever. Dengue Fever. Malaria. Swine Flu. Water you daren't drink, food you daren't eat. I'd always assumed my trip to Brazil for one concert would end up being cancelled, and it's only now as I leaf through a tourist book in the airport while waiting for the flight that I realise the implications of what I'm letting myself in for.

It wasn't just me that had doubts about this gig happening. I'll be supporting Sham 69, and when I met them at the check-in desk they seemed as surprised as me when they actually got handed the boarding cards. For Sham there's quite a history to this gig: they were supposed to play Sao Paulo three years ago but had some internal problems that resulted in them kicking original singer Jimmy Pursey out of the band. After that they brought in a new singer Tim V (not the Tim V writing this, though in fact they did invite me to join them.) The gig was rescheduled for a year later, but just then the global recession hit and the promoters had to cancel because the Brazilian currency nose-dived. This then is Sham's third attempt to get to Brazil, and this time I'm coming too.

24th September

The first people I meet on arrival in Brazil are two nurses in masks who take my swine flu declaration card from me, not actually checking to see that I hadn't bothered to fill it out.

After a thirteen hour flight arriving at five in the morning the chaos of Sao Paulo airport is hard to take, particularly for original Sham guitarist Dave Parsons, who finds his bag doesn't come up on the carousel and has to go to the lost luggage desk to organise getting it sent on to our hotel if it should turn up.

Then there are long queues to get through customs and into the arrivals hall where promoter Renato is waiting for us, concerned that it's taken an hour since the plane landed before we came through. We bundle into the waiting van and hit the traffic-clogged motorway into town, gawping at the raggedy pile of shanty town on the right. Renato tells us that it's the last remaining one, the rest have been torn down and the inhabitants moved out into proper homes.

We've hit the morning rush hour, and it takes over an hour to get to the hotel. At first we edge bumper to bumper down the motorway, then the massive tangled skyscraper maze of Sao Paulo swallows us up, the cars swerving and changing lanes at high speed through the bumpy and disordered city streets, where red lights are considered more of a challenge than an instruction. At the hotel, the rooms aren't ready yet – hard to believe after being awake so long that it's still only nine in the morning – but breakfast is still available in the hotel breakfast room and Renato leads us all in there, heads down like tired sheep, to chat about what will be happening over the next few days and get something to eat. I'm pleased about that as I'm very hungry: Iberia Airlines seem to confuse being a vegetarian with being on a diet.

Over coffee Renato hands out some printed sheets and we go through today's schedule. 14:00 is Lunch Time – well, I'll skip that after all this breakfast. At 18:00 I'll be rehearsing with a local band who have learnt six of my songs ready for the gig. At 21:30 it's 'Dinner at *Carneceria Z*' – um, may be skipping that too. Then at midnight we'll be going to a club called Vegas where Dave and I are going to do DJ sets of our ten favourite songs from CDs that we've prepared in England. Just two problems here: Dave's CD is in the bag that didn't arrive, and Renato didn't tell me about this idea before so I have nothing.

It's now 10:30 and we're told the rooms are ready. Renato asks me to scribble out a list of songs – he'll try and find them to download during the day – then Sham and I troop off upstairs. I dump my bags and take a shower, then go for a walk up the road to try and get a taste of the city. The weather is disappointingly grey and cold. Run-down two storey shops and boarded-up houses line each side of the street, while high rise blocks pile up behind as far as the eye can see. The city is immense. Six million people, and most of them seem to be on this street. Despite all the reports of pickpockets and street crime, I actually feel quite safe.

At six I head over to the Inferno club, where we'll be playing in two days, to meet Joe, club co-owner and guitarist in my soon-to-be band. He and the other owner Leandro sit me down and insist we have a beer together while we wait for Renato. Joe tells me we have time booked in one of the best rehearsal rooms in the city this evening. The best drummer in town I'd been promised isn't available so the bass player has found another one. Joe admits that he's never actually played with the bass player or the replacement drummer before, but he's heard they're good and have been learning the songs. Joe himself has been practicing and says he is ready to go, but all the same this is somewhat less than the ready-rehearsed band I had been promised.

The rehearsal room is only about a mile away but it takes us ninety minutes to get there, a giddying ride through the streets now clogged with traffic trying to leave the city. 'Welcome to the jungle!' says Renato.

Eventually we reach the rehearsal complex and Joe takes me through to the well-appointed, spacious room we'll be using and introduces me to the bassist. There's a drum kit set up in the middle of the room and a guy sat quietly behind it obviously ready to start, his girlfriend sitting on the floor behind him. I go over and introduce myself and ask him, 'So, how are you feeling about the songs – are you confident?'

He looks at me blankly.

Uh oh – he speaks *no* English.

Renato comes in. 'I don't believe it! My son is practicing with a band in one of the other rooms!'

We run through the first number. Considering we're in one of the best rehearsal rooms in the city the sound is atrocious. It's loud, but piercingly shrill, and despite the volume the song is sounding completely unexciting, though I find it hard to put my finger on exactly why.

'So, how was it?' Joe asks keenly as the last note dies down.

'Wellll, I'm not sure.'

He looks crushed. After aborted attempts at two more songs I realise what's wrong: the drummer is playing like a robot. There's no life in it. Even worse, when I try and get him to speed the songs up a bit, he picks up the pace for a while then gradually slows back down to his original tempo. When I ask him to play even faster, he keeps the beat up but it sounds ridiculous, like a record at the wrong speed.

I have to leave the room to clear my head for a moment. Suddenly the thirty hours I've been awake is crushing down on me. Joe rushes out after me. 'What is it?'

I turn to him. 'I – I just can't play with this drummer. He has no feel.'

'I knew it! This is not my guy! I'm going to fix it! I can get another drummer…!'

I feel my knees go weak at the thought of having to teach a drummer six songs he's never heard before. Joe goes off to talk to Renato and I slouch back into the rehearsal room, give the drummer an apologetic shrug, and sit on the carpet in front of the kit while he laboriously packs away his sticks and cymbals, every resentful ring of wing nut and zip of stick bag tearing an accusatory hole in the silence. Then his girlfriend gets up and they leave. I shake his hand and apologise as he goes, but he clearly thinks I am a complete bastard.

When Joe returns I say, 'I don't think it's going to be possible to teach a new drummer all these songs he's never tried before. We only have one day. Why don't I just do a solo set?'

'The drummer is on his way! He'll be here in ten minutes!'

It turns out to be a guy called Jeff, the drummer in his regular band and also his flatmate. I already know this is not going to work but watch with sinking heart as Joe tries to explain how the first song goes and Jeff sits behind the kit and taps a couple of beats out, wrongly, in response to Joe's hand movements.

It's with some amazement that thirty seconds into the song I realise it's all starting to click. The guy is hungry, it's obvious – he's beating shit out of the drums, and even though some of the subtleties of the songs are missing, this guy has got it. It might just work. I go over to his stool at the end of the song and give him a hug. He is already soaked with sweat from the effort he's put into just this one song.

'Thank you for saving the gig,' I say, and the whole room breathes a collective sigh of relief.

Then Jeff goes over to the sound desk and fiddles with a few knobs and suddenly the P.A. sounds great too. 'He was supposed to be the sound man for the gig, but now we're going to have to find someone else,' says Joe.

It takes another two hours to work through the rest of the songs. By the end of that, Jeff looks as tired as I feel. There's no way we're going to get anything more constructive done today, but it turns out that the bass player has a studio of his own so we arrange to rehearse again tomorrow – and I say goodbye to my day off. What time shall we start?

'Twelve!' says Joe.

'Well, how about two,' I say.

'Three?' says Jeff.

Back into traffic for the long drive back to the hotel. I drop the guitar off in my room and meet up with Sham outside. It's now past eleven and time to head up the road to the Vegas club for the DJ sets. I missed the scheduled dinner at 21:30, but Tim V – who's also vegetarian – tells me that despite the name, the *Carneceria* did have a veggie burger on the menu. He says it was quite nice, 'a kind of a mush in a bun' with stuffed vine leaves for a starter.

The Vegas club is just preparing to open as we arrive. The staff are still getting the bar ready but Renato gets everyone a beer and we stand around self-consciously as the floor is cleaned around us, not really knowing what to do. Renato suggests to me that we could go out for something to eat now, but the *Carneceria* is shut, so I end up with a warm bread roll with some griddled cheese in it at a café next door. Bread and cheese on tour – well, that makes a nice change!

By the time the club has filled it's getting on for two and Dave and I are both tired and not really in the mood to do the DJ spot, so when Renato comes over to tell us it's time to start it's with some reluctance that we get on the small stage with the guy who's going to be working the decks for us. He doesn't speak English and starts off with a few of Dave's tracks before he realises we're supposed to be taking it in turn. I make an unconvincing attempt to do that thing DJ's do, looking like they're having the best party in the world, while Dave sits on the sofa behind the decks, drinking a beer, and slopes off as soon as the records are over, leaving me on my own to play the rest of mine. I cut a few out from the list and get the hell off the stage. Some guy shakes my hand as I go past, 'You're a great DJ man!'

Eh?

We go with Joe back down the road to his club where he gets us a couple more beers and then takes me up to his office so we can get away from the music and chill out for a while. But pretty soon everyone he knows has followed us up there. Aware of the fact that it's now nearly five – that would be nine in the morning U.K. time – I soon slip off back downstairs and head for the hotel. I'm pretty pleased with myself that despite the bad reputation of the mean streets of Sao Paulo, and despite my rather large intake of alcohol this evening, I find my way back on my own unscathed. Mind you, the hotel is literally next door.

25th September

At seven in the morning my mobile phone rings. I grasp around for it. 'Hello?' I say thickly. A bright and breezy voice sounds in my ear, 'Good morning! This is Dave from Quay West Radio, Somerset. We'd arranged to do an interview now, eleven o'clock?'

Indeed we had. Next week. In England.

Soon after that the noise of the road being dug up outside starts and, unable to sleep through it, I decide to go down for breakfast, arriving five minutes before it finishes at 9:55. There is only one other person in the room, a businessman in his late fifties, and I notice how every time he comes back from the buffet he sits down one place nearer to me. Eventually he is only one seat away and the conversation starts. 'I noticed you come in yesterday – you are with a band?'

He was a musician too when he was younger. He was in England a few years ago, working on some defence project. I start to get interested and try and wheedle some more information out of him, but he's not giving out much. He tells me he is now working on a housing project in Angola. That's where all the money is to be made at the moment, rebuilding the infrastructure, and all the foreign companies are moving in trying to get a slice of it. 'Hilary Clinton was there a couple of weeks ago, lobbying for it,' he says. 'But she didn't get it. *I* got it.'

I have the day free until the rehearsal at three so I go out for another long walk, this time down the hill to the city centre and onwards. It's a great feeling to wander aimlessly around a new place, tempered only by the pollution that makes me feel I'm going down with a head cold. I get a bit lost but make it back to the hotel by 2:30. From my room I email Joe to find out where we're going to meet, but he replies that Renato is still at the studio with Sham so rehearsal is now going to be more like five. At six I get a text from Renato to say he's in Reception with Sham and we're going to go for something to eat, we can go to rehearse after that.

As we walk up the road, Tim V complains that the pollution is making him feel like he has been punched in the nose. I ask him about the radio session this morning and he tells me that when they got to the studio there were no cymbals for the drum kit and they had to wait around four hours before some arrived so they could start.

'Four hours?! I hope they gave you something to eat and drink in the meantime!'

'Well, after two hours some woman came in with some biscuits,'

The restaurant Renato intends to take us to isn't actually open yet – it's only seven and no Brazilian in their right minds would eat this early – so we end up as the only diners in an all-day café further up the street, where I get a kind of vegetable pizza. Kind of.

Then we go back down the hill to the hotel. Sham go to their rooms for a post-prandial rest, and I get in the car with Renato to head for rehearsal. Even as we reverse out into the street from the hotel forecourt, I realise what's going to happen. Traffic.

Traffic.

You swing down the side streets, you take the short cuts, you swerve into the slow lane, squeeze into impossible gaps and take impossible risks but nothing will get you there any quicker. If you get into a car for any reason in Sao Paulo, put your life on hold.

An hour after we set off, we pick Joe and Jeff up from outside their apartment. 'Hey, Tim, I brought you a beer,' says Joe as he climbs in. 'Ice cold!'

It's a help, but it still takes almost another hour before we pull out of the traffic onto a side street that winds up to a hill overlooking the city where the bass player has his studio. Very nice it is too, much more pleasant than the expensive professional one – and his mum lives downstairs and brings up a thermos of potent sweet black coffee for us, which we drink out of tiny plastic cups.

We run through the set again and everything sounds pretty good. I even allow myself to feel confident. 'Okay, let's take a break and then go through them again,' says Joe as the last song finishes.

'Do you want to see my snakes?' says the bass player.

Not a question I'd expected, but I follow him up the steps to the kitchen where there are a couple of tanks, one with some pythons and another one with some snakes with pink markings. 'Corn snakes,' he says.

'And you're sure they're not poisonous?' I ask, as he gently drapes one over my hands.

Then we go back downstairs and run through the set again and it sounds great. Once again I say thank you to Jeff and tell him what a great job he's doing, standing in at the last minute like this. I read out something written in marker pen on his cymbals – *vai Molina vai!* – and everyone in the room laughs. Jeff's surname is Molina, and he's written *Go, Molina, go!* to inspire himself when he's playing. I tell him I'm going to say that on stage when we start tomorrow.

Renato phones up the hotel to arrange to meet up with Sham when we get back, but there's no reply from their rooms and he looks a bit worried about the idea of them out on their own somewhere in the big city. Personally, seeing how tired they were earlier, I think they're asleep. We're all tired too. Joe says he didn't get much sleep last night because after I left the club he met this girl and, well, he doesn't seem to have his underwear any more.

Back into the traffic. I sit in the front with Renato and he tells me about some of the bands he's brought to Sao Paulo in the past. He used to put them up in a four star hotel in the city centre, he tells me, but the area started to get dangerous – there was a street down the side of the hotel that started to fill up with crack heads and drug dealers at night and the police don't go anywhere near. 'That'll be where Sham are!' I say brightly.

On we go, and it occurs to me that the most conversation I've had since I've been here has taken place during car journeys – you might as well relax and forget about the clock because you never know how long it will take to get where you are going.

Joe asks if there's anything I want at the gig tomorrow. 'Just let me know. If you want food, something special to drink?'

'Naked women…?' says Renato.

'Oh, okay, I'll have two of them. Three.'

Joe's voice floats over from the back seat. 'Actually, I could arrange that…'

I think he means it.

'You have to come again,' Joe continues. 'Next time you will have to have a day off at the beach.'

I turn to Renato, raising an eyebrow. 'A day off? What's that?'

Joe brushes it aside. 'You are going to have a day off,' he insists. 'There is a perfect beach just a couple of hours away. We are going to go there and I am going to make you smoke weed and drink *Caipirinha*. You are going to be a Rasta!'

We drive through the centre, past a luxury hotel with a sordid looking street beside it, a few unsavoury characters hanging around. 'Is that the street you were talking about?' I ask Renato, and he nods.

'Just drop me off here,' I say, 'I'll find my own way back to the hotel.'

But actually, the hotel isn't an option yet. It's only midnight. Still unable to raise any of Sham 69 on the phone, we head up the road to another club, where an old Sao Paulo punk band will be playing later. Joe is by my side as we walk. 'See that place over there,' he says, pointing across the road, 'You can openly buy cocaine there and the police do nothing, but if you smoke a cigarette in my club they will close me down!'

Off the main street and down a side road and we are at the club. The band aren't going to be onstage until two, but right now there's a DJ playing some great Sixties tracks. One of the guys in the band comes over and tells me what an honour it is to meet me. 'The Advjeerts,' he says. 'Gary Moore, my favourite guitarist.'

I have no idea what he's talking about.

It's been a long couple of days and it's getting a bit claustrophobic in the rapidly-filling club, but where Joe goes doors open, and we escape to an upstairs room to get some air and a quiet beer. Quite a few other people follow us up there and pretty soon the place is buzzing. I'm sitting next to a friend of Joe's called Camilla, who has a striking tattoo right across her chest and is telling me how she has just moved back to Sao Paulo after living for some years in London.

'London seems slow compared to this,' I say.

She says, 'Welcome to the jungle.'

We chat some more and then I happen to look over and notice Joe and another guy sitting on the other side of the table, Joe in his off-the-peg red tartan punk trousers and the other guy in a pair with an eye-boggling two tone geometric pattern he has clearly designed himself. I break off the conversation. 'That has got to be the best two pairs of trousers that have ever been in one room together!' I exclaim.

'I knew you were gay,' says Camilla to the room.

She turns back to me, chuckling. 'We have a saying in Brazil: *lose your friends, but never lose a joke.*'

Back downstairs the band is starting up. I listen to a couple of numbers but it's now four in the morning and after the rehearsal and the long day I'm full of music and can't take any more. Renato has been keeping an eye on me, and now suggests it might be time he took me back to the hotel. 'You don't need to worry about that,' I say, 'I can find my own way.'

Although, when I get outside, it occurs to me that I'm not sure if we turned left or right off *Rua Augusto* to get here. I could try going up there to the next main street, I'm sure I'd recognise it, but on the other hand it could take a while if I'm wrong, and it has got awfully late…

I decide to swallow my pride and go back to the club and find Renato, but the woman on the door says she can't let me in. I'm just mulling this over, when Renato steps out and gestures me to follow him. He sets off in the opposite direction to the one I was going to try and ten minutes later we're heading down *Augusto*, past the dark, sleazy and dangerous-looking crack joint that Joe pointed out earlier. 'You go on,' I say to Renato, 'I'll find my way from here.'

26th September

There's still time for a walk when I eventually wake up, and today the sun is even peeking out occasionally. When it does, Sao Paulo makes sense. I watch some kids doing some street gymnastics, including some improbable and extremely dangerous jumps from a high wall behind a disused fountain by the metro station. The pollution seems to be affecting me even worse than yesterday and it occurs to me that, embarrassingly, as I wander around constantly sniffing and swiping at my nose, I must look like the typical English coke tourist.

At five-thirty I go to the club. Sham are on the stage and in mid-soundcheck, Dave already in his suit ready for the gig as the bag with his stage clothes finally arrived from the airport this afternoon. Jeff is upstairs doing the sound and trying to get to grips with the club's new digital mixing desk, the first time it has ever been used. Consequently it takes a little while before everything is right, but then he soundchecks my voice and guitar for the solo part of my set and it's all done in a couple of minutes. Finally the last-minute replacement sound man takes over and Jeff rushes down the steps and gets behind the drum kit to soundcheck as part of my band. We run through most of the songs and everything is sounding good.

After that he heads back upstairs to set up the sound for the local band who'll be on first, and then there's a lot of waiting around, always pretty much the same no matter what continent you're on. Jeff sits in the backstage room with me and tells me how much he is enjoying all this. Right now he needs something positive to focus on: two days ago, the day he got called in to play drums for me, his father got diagnosed with cancer and he's been spending a lot of time visiting him in hospital.

He also tells me that he came to England once. Not for long though. At Immigration they asked how long he intended to stay, and he told them, one month. Then they asked him how much money he had, and he showed them the thousand U.S. dollars he had with him. 'That's not enough,' they said, locked him up overnight and sent him back to Brazil the next day.

My scheduled start time of ten approaches but I think we can forget the schedule – we are in Brazil and it's a Saturday night. The local band hasn't even got on stage yet. The club is filling up nicely though, and eventually the first band begin. They are a high energy indie/punk band, and from where I'm sitting backstage they sound pretty good, but when they finish the first song no one at all claps. Sham and I look at each other in disbelief. 'Tough crowd,' I say.

I had expected a lively and wild audience in Brazil, but Joe tells me that this is normal – the support band is just on as filler, and no one is supposed to give them any appreciation. Strange but true – because when I start putting my stuff on stage I get cheered for just standing there.

I stand there for longer than I expected, actually, because the DJ seems reluctant to stop playing records, and when I can finally start, the guitar immediately cuts out and the stage box it plugs into has to be changed, so it's not quite the explosive beginning to my first ever gig in Brazil I'd hoped for. It does however give a chance for someone in the audience to shout out 'Generation Y!' I'd never expected anyone here to know anything other than Adverts songs, so when he calls for it again, and the girl next to him shouts 'Beautiful song!' I play it.

Eight songs in and it's time to introduce the band. *Vai Molina, vai!*

They play their hearts out and despite a few mistakes and more technical problems near the end when a string breaks on Joe's guitar, closely followed by the strap, it's a lot of fun.

Don't think the night ends there. It's only two in the morning, and after I've taken my guitar back to the hotel room I will be required to get in the car and be driven to another club that Renato recommends and I won't be getting out of there until five in the morning again, even then disappointing the girl who is driving and intends to go on to the Vegas club after she drops me off at the hotel. She used to own it and has lots of friends there. I have to say, despite the thirteen hour flight tomorrow, I'm tempted. Even though it's Sunday morning, it's still Saturday night. Maybe it's always Saturday night here.

Ah, Sao Paulo. I've been here three days and all my life.

6. THE JOY OF TRAVEL (2009)

24th December

Dear Sirs,

Following our earlier phone conversation, I am writing with details of my recent trips to ascertain what travel insurance payments will be appropriate.

I am a musician and have recently completed a thirty-three date tour of Europe. After the first 27 gigs I had taken a couple of days break at home and was booked on a BA flight from London Heathrow to Zurich on December 17th for the last few concerts. I was due to play in Winterthur that night, then go on to two further gigs in Switzerland and one in Southern Germany over the next three days, flying back from Zurich to London on the 21st December. On the following day, the 22nd December, I was booked on a BA flight from London to Frankfurt, to play a private birthday party engagement, returning home the following day, 23rd December.

My problems began a couple of weeks before my trip, when BA cabin crew announced a strike, due to start on 23rd December. This put my concert at the birthday party at risk because there was no guarantee I would be able to get home the next day. I contacted the person who had booked me for his party and we agreed to wait until BA announced its alternative schedule before deciding what to do. We hoped that there was still a chance that the strike would be called off, or even if it went ahead, that my flight would not be one of those affected.

Unfortunately BA decided not to announce its alternative schedule until a judgement had been given on a legal challenge they had made against the union, and this had still not happened on the day I was due to fly to Zurich. The person organising the party contacted me that morning and asked me to buy a Lufthansa single ticket from Frankfurt to London for the day after the party to be sure I could get home in case of a strike. He couldn't risk me not coming because 150 guests were expected and the venue and PA system had already been hired. I then bought this ticket at a price of €207. An hour later the BA strike was ruled illegal and called off. Please advise me if I can make a claim for the price of the unnecessary ticket.

After booking the new ticket, I left home at 13:30 to catch the Underground to Heathrow, a journey which usually takes around forty minutes. My flight to Zurich was not scheduled to depart until 15:50 so I was still in good time but unfortunately I then had a forty minute wait at Acton Town station for a Terminal Five train. London Underground tell me that this was due to an earlier signal failure and will refund my tube fare, so I do not need to claim this from you, but the result was that I arrived at Terminal Five with only five minutes to spare to clear Security. Even though I had already checked in online the attendant told me that she could not let me on the flight. I showed her my printout which stated I still had five minutes to spare but she told me the flight closed 'automatically' and she was unable to do anything about it. She advised me to go the BA help desk.

At the BA help desk I was informed that I would have to buy another ticket to Zurich. There were still two available flights that day: one from Heathrow at 19:15, and one from London City at 18:30. Given the one hour time difference between London and Zurich, I judged that I would have a better chance of getting to my gig if I took the earlier flight – even though it was ten pounds more expensive and would mean me taking a two hour journey across London to the other airport. I paid the £163.20 and received a printout confirming that I was booked on this flight. As London Underground admit that my delay getting to the airport was due to them, I would like to claim for the cost of this ticket.

At this point I sent an SMS to my friend René in Switzerland, who had booked the gig for me, and told him what had happened. I was now due to arrive in Zurich at 21:10, so although I would certainly miss soundcheck there seemed a good chance I could be at the venue shortly after ten, still in time to play the gig.

I then took the Underground and Docklands Light Railway to London City airport. Please advise me if this expense is covered by my travel insurance.

At London City I was able to check in for my new flight, but the BA person asked me if I was aware that as I had missed my outward flight from Heathrow, it was normal policy for the return flight to be cancelled. I told her that I was not aware of this. She told me that I should go to the BA help desk opposite.

At the BA help desk, I explained that I still wanted to use the return part of the ticket, but I was told that return flights are cancelled 'automatically' and nothing could be done about it. Eventually I phoned up BA Customer Relations, where I was also told that my return flight would have been cancelled. However, when the lady on the phone checked on her computer she informed me that the ticket desk at Heathrow had actually marked it as confirmed. She told me, 'They shouldn't have done that.'

After a long queue to get through Security I saw on the Departure Boards that my flight was delayed by 30 minutes. I relayed the information to René and he told me that he would pick me up from Zurich airport when I arrived and drive me straight to Winterthur, so we could still be at the venue shortly after eleven. I would still be in time for the concert but would have to play a bit shorter than usual. When I looked back at the Departure Boards, they showed a one hour delay.

There was now heavy snow falling. I checked the live travel news and saw that my original flight from Heathrow had arrived an hour late on its inbound leg to London, so I could easily have checked in for if I had been allowed to. My new flight was now showing a one hour fifty minute delay.

I sent a text to René to tell him that there now seemed to be no chance I would make it in time for the gig, but shortly afterwards he replied that he had been in contact with the venue and they had said that the place was packed and if necessary I could start the concert at midnight. At around 20:00 our plane arrived at the stand and soon after that we began boarding. By the revised departure time of 20:30 we were in our seats. After another twenty minutes, the captain announced that we were unable to take off yet because the runway needed to be cleared of snow, which would take between 30 to 60 minutes.

There was now clearly no chance that I would arrive in Winterthur in time for my concert, and after an hour the captain announced that all further flights out of London City had been cancelled and we should leave the plane and rebook for tomorrow. I would like to claim the standard 12 hour departure delay on my travel insurance.

While I was in the queue at the BA help desk to rebook, it occurred to me that if I didn't take my return flight from Zurich to London on the 21st, I could play the Winterthur gig that day instead. The following day I could take a train to Frankfurt to play at the birthday party instead of flying from London to Frankfurt. As I wouldn't have used the outward part of my London to Frankfurt BA ticket, the return part would probably get cancelled, but I still had the reserve Lufthansa single ticket I'd bought in case of the BA strike. The only extra cost would be the price of the train ticket from Zurich to Frankfurt. René relayed this information to the venue and they announced from the stage that I would be arriving on Monday. Please advise if I can charge for the price of the additional train fare.

I enclose all the necessary documents with this letter. The details of the replacement flight out of Heathrow on the 18th are handwritten on a scrap of paper because when I arrived at the BA help desk there was a power failure and they were unable to use their printer.

Yours sincerely,

Tim Smith

31st December

Dear Tom,

Thanks for your email and the photos. It's good to hear that your guests enjoyed my performance at your birthday party!

Thanks also for dropping me off at the station the next day. You might be interested to know that I got to Frankfurt airport early so I thought I would go to the BA check-in desk and see if it was still possible to use the return portion of my ticket even though I hadn't used the outward flight. I didn't really expect them to let me on, but to my surprise they did so I was home two hours earlier than expected.

When I arrived home, Gaye told me that on the day of your party all BA flights from London to the rest of Europe were cancelled due to the bad weather. That means, *if* my flight to Switzerland on the 17th hadn't been cancelled, and *if* I consequently hadn't moved the Winterthur gig to the 21st, I would have flown home that day as planned and then found that the flight out to Frankfurt on the 22nd was cancelled, which means I would have been unable to get there to play your birthday.

So everything worked out perfectly!

Happy New Year!

Tim

7. SLIPPY (2010)

After so many gigs lately you'd think everything would be running like clockwork, but ever since I missed that flight to Switzerland a few weeks ago things keep happening that I can't seem to get a grip on. Life is getting slippy.

Why, only last weekend I was booked for two gigs that were virtually just down the road. I've played the lovely Steamboat in Ipswich countless times and it's only an hour away on the train. As usual I book the tickets on the Trainline website in advance but when I get to Liverpool Street and put in the booking code, the machine only prints the return ticket. Still ten minutes before the train leaves so I hurry into the booking office only to find a long queue. By the time I get to the counter my train has gone and the guy there refuses to give me another ticket. He insists that it's impossible for the machine to only print one part of the ticket – I must have left the other part in it. I say I didn't. He says I have to ring up Trainline because it must be their mistake putting two tickets on one booking code – that's always happening, that's why they don't deal with Trainline any more, etc, etc.

I refuse to leave the counter because I know I will never get a ticket from this guy if I do and there is clearly no way internet-only Trainline will do anything, even if I can get through to them. To my surprise, I do get through, but only to an Indian call centre. There is a two second delay and an echo on the line and the person I am speaking to can't understand what I am saying. It takes five or six goes just for her to get my name right, then we attempt to establish the booking code. Then the 'security questions'. After a long discussion during which I am put on hold a number of times while she talks to her supervisor, she finally tells me that Trainline can't take responsibility because their computers show I have picked up the tickets. There must be a fault with the machine, which belongs to the train company. I tell this to the guy behind the counter and he beckons for me to give him the phone and then has a similarly lengthy and fruitless discussion. Eventually he gives me back the phone, sighs, draws a pad of travel vouchers from under his desk, fills one out and hands it to me. When I'm on the train at last and heading for my no-doubt-to-be-without-soundcheck gig – and yes, it was the night where the PA didn't work properly and if we'd had a soundcheck we might have been able to fix it – I look at the voucher and see there are a number of checkboxes for the reason for issue. One of the checkboxes is: 'Ticket machine only dispensed part of the ticket,' but the guy hasn't ticked that one, he's ticked 'Other.'

And then there was Sheerness the next day, where the train didn't go where it was supposed to according to the timetable and so I had to change twice more than I was expecting to and the person whose birthday gig I was playing drank so much vodka that he kept falling over in the venue. 'My Dad's not supposed to get drunk,' his daughter told me. 'He's got epilepsy.' I was staying the night at the family's house, and most of the audience ended up there too. I had been warned that the place was a bit of a mess because recently the hot water boiler fell though the ceiling but I hadn't expected to find a 'drum kit set up in the kitchen, and was also surprised when the guy's son started thrashing away at it at three in the morning, much to the rowdy delight of all the other guests. My bedroom was directly above it and was also the room the boiler had landed in. I was going down with a cold at the time and spent a couple of hours snuffling and shivering in my coat while the party went on around me until someone I'd never met before took pity on me and offered me the spare room at his place. I ended up there eventually and it was nice and quiet, though unfortunately without heating so I slept in my clothes. The next day the guy drove me to a station further down the line so that I could avoid the extra changes, but the line was closed for engineering works anyway so I had to wait for the bus replacement. A vehicle that looked like it hadn't been started up since the fifties rattled the scenic way through most of Kent before dumping me at a station somewhere which didn't have a café. Neither did the train. I hadn't had time to get a drink before we left the house and was so thirsty by now that I was seeing oases across the Medway flats. When I finally got in to Victoria...

Well, I think you get the idea.

Then a one-off in Germany, a duo gig with Vom in Düsseldorf. We always have a great time doing these, the venue is sure to be packed and I'm really looking forward to it. Just before I leave for the airport, Vom suggests getting a friend of ours, Thomas, to play guest guitar on the set. He was in a band with Vom and me when we did a short tour in Germany a couple of years ago so he probably still knows most of the songs. Three other bands are on the bill tonight and there's no time for us to get a soundcheck by the time they've all finished, so we go backstage, sit around and rehearse the songs acoustically.

Everything sounds great but there's still a long wait before we play. We are in a good mood. We have a few beers, and Vom and I start thinking of a few routines we could do on the stage. We've taken to going on carrying daft Vic'n'Bob-style handbags – tonight we've even bought a spare one for Thomas – and now we prepare them by filling them with various items from the dressing room buffet: mainly beer, but also some fruit, oranges, bananas and grapes, which we'll no doubt find some reason to whip out during the course of the show. Then we draw some stupid faces on paper plates, make a nose hole to attach them, some eye holes to see out of, and scheme to make our grand rock'n'roll entrance to the stage wearing them. It's a birthday party, why not have a laugh?

Finally the other bands have finished. It's getting near midnight now, so we hurry up to the stage to set our gear up, planning to come back to the dressing room to get the face plates when all the technical stuff is sorted out. On the far side of the stage, Thomas seems to have his guitar working, it's blasting out of the monitors over there. My guitar, however, isn't working at all. The sound guy gets up on to the stage and changes over a few cables and the D.I. box but still nothing's coming through. Thomas and Vom are both ready now, and we decide to go back to the dressing room while the soundman sorts things out. At least we can grab the handbags and a beer. After ten minutes there's still no word from the soundman. Knowing there is a sold out venue waiting for us, we decide to put on the face plates and fool around on stage while the technical problems are being fixed – at least it will keep the audience entertained. Peering through my little eye holes, I am quite surprised to see the soundman hanging around by the stage entrance. I thought he would be dashing around getting things working. I stop by his side and tell him what we are planning to do.

'There is a little problem,' he says.

'Really?' I say. 'What's that?'

'I broke your guitar.'

'Pardon?'

'I just broke your guitar. On the stage.'

I go up to the stage, where my guitar is lying in two pieces in front of one of the amps. I take off the face plate.

My guitar. Hand built by my brother, custom designed for playing live, extra struts and strengthening to stop feedback, thin-bodied to make it lighter to carry, the wood hand-picked. The guitar I've played at every gig for the last fifteen years. More than a thousand hours on stage, my last four records…

I am still reeling as Thomas rushes past. 'Play mine,' he says, 'I will get an electric.'

As Vom goes past to the drum kit, I tell him, 'I don't think I can do the handbags tonight.'

I hold up the pieces of my guitar to the audience to show them what has happened and strap on the one Thomas hands me. Unfortunately the strap is very short and can't be adjusted so the thing hangs somewhere just below my neck and bangs painfully against my ribs for the entire gig. Presumably the soundman is in denial about having broken my guitar, because the sound from this one is still coming though the monitor on the far side of the stage in front of Thomas, there's absolutely nothing coming through the one in front of me. Vom can't hear anything either from where he is up on the drum riser and at one point between songs I see him hurling the drum monitor across the stage. The electric guitar Thomas is using sounds so awful that he has to run off and borrow a different one. But somehow we get through it. The audience is with us, singing along and applauding and the atmosphere is electric for the whole hour, but somehow I feel far away…my guitar…my rock…gone. In two days I'm supposed to be on tour in Finland. It feels like the ground is shifting out from under my feet. Slippy.

9th February

As soon as I got home from Germany I sent my brother photos of the guitar and he reckons he can fix it. Yesterday I packed it up and sent it down to Brook Guitars, his workshop in Devon. The only other guitar I own is an electric, a Fender Telecaster which, ironically, I part-exchanged for my spare acoustic just a couple of months ago. I've never played an electric guitar at a solo gig before but I don't have much choice now. I don't even own an amp and cabinet and couldn't carry them if I did, but I'll take an effects unit and hope for the best.

The trouble is, when life gets slippy, it's hard to predict which way it will slip next. For example, my itinerary only arrived from Rowan at the booking agency yesterday afternoon and I've been so busy with the guitar that I haven't had time to read it through properly – who knows what nasty surprises lie in store? I know there are a lot of train journeys involved and quite a few early starts. I've also got a fairly early flight to Finland this morning and I've had so many delays on the public transport system lately that I take a taxi to Heathrow just to be certain I will be on time. But it turns out that there has been an accident on the motorway; we crawl along at almost walking pace and it takes more than an hour to get to the airport, longer than the tube would have taken. By the time I rush up to the British Airways check-in desk I am in danger of missing the flight, and overheating under all the clothes I am wearing ready for Finland where the weather forecast shows it will be extremely cold. For some reason I hadn't been able to check in online like I usually do, and one of the BA staff explains why: this is a codeshare flight, and I am actually flying on Finnair. Unfortunately, Finnair has a different luggage policy to BA, and at the check-in desk they tell me that I will not be allowed to take the guitar on board. Even more unfortunate, the Telecaster only has a soft case so if it does have to go in the hold with the rest of the luggage it's sure to get damaged. So there is a lengthy argument. With great reluctance, the check-in woman finally agrees to let me take the guitar with me to the gate, but she tells me it will almost certainly be taken away from me when I get there. Well, let's get that far at least, I think: one step at a time.

At the gate, the same women is seated behind the desk, and I see her exchange glances with her colleague who is checking boarding cards beside her. 'I've already alerted them,' she says under her breath.

I take a seat in the lounge with the rest of the passengers, and a couple of minutes later there is an announcement over the loudspeaker: 'We remind passengers that only *one item* of hand luggage per person is allowed. If you have *more than one item* please make yourself known to the staff. Passengers are informed that if they go to the aircraft with *more than one item* it will not be allowed on board and will have to be left behind.'

Yes, I'm getting the message.

But I'm not going to officially report my extra luggage to the staff as they are clearly already aware of it. When the flight is called I jump up and get near the front of the queue, well placed to be one of the first on board before the luggage racks fill up too much. It is not to be: the Finnair woman comes up, takes me to one side and says, 'Could you sit down again, sir. We are going to board all the other passengers first and then see if there is room for your guitar at the end.'

So, while the room empties I sit alone in the lounge, feeling like a criminal. Five minutes pass, ten minutes…the Finnair women have vacated their desk. For all I know, the plane has already taken off. I'm starting to get nervous, thinking they have forgotten me. Then suddenly the woman who checked me in is back.

'The crew say you can take your guitar on board,' she says.

Of course they do. They always do. It's only you bastards who always try and stop me.

On the flight I can finally relax, and there's time to leaf through the English-language *Helsinki Times*. Much of the news concerns the weather: Finland is experiencing a very severe winter with near-record snowfall wreaking havoc on Helsinki's transport system. They are running out of places to dump the excess snow as it is cleared, and in parts of the city streets are becoming alarmingly narrow.

After we land we have to wait an hour for the luggage to come up on the carousel. Some sort of strike, apparently. Looks like I will be a little bit late for soundcheck, but at least I have my guitar with me so I'm reasonably unworried about the situation. The Finnish guy sitting next to me, on the other hand, is grumbling and muttering to himself. After a while he goes over and remonstrates with the staff, then comes back to his seat and turns to me: 'I told them you were very angry about having to wait so long.'

Me?

The airport bus takes me into the centre of Helsinki, right next to the railway station, and I'm tempted to drop in there and pick up my pre-booked train tickets for the rest of the tour, but soundcheck time is fast approaching and I want to dump my suitcase in the hotel first. It's going to be a slog carrying everything through the snow. My hotel is one of the plush Sokos chain and I've stayed there before, so I set off through the snow-packed streets confident I'll find it. It's a big building with its name in lights on the top of it, after all, and I know I'm heading in more or less the right direction. But after fifteen minutes I still can't see it anywhere. Worried about soundcheck I decide to leave out the guesswork, and instead go back down to the station to ask directions in the other Sokos hotel there, just opposite from where the bus dropped me off. At the Reception desk there they circle my hotel on a tourist map, just one corner away from where I gave up.

I unpack my bags in my room, and although I really should be going to soundcheck, the need to pick up the tickets is nagging at me. I have to get an early train to Tampere tomorrow, and from there tour agent Harri will pick me up and drive me to Virrat. If I don't get the tickets until the morning I'll need to be at the station at around nine in case of any problems – I'm thinking, *Trainline* – and at that time it will be crammed with commuters and there will be long queues at the desks and the ticket machines. To get there at nine I'll need to wake up at eight, and given the two hour time difference with the UK that will feel like six. And tonight is sure to be a late one. So I decide to go to the station on the way to the club; it's only a small detour and it's going to be bothering me all night if I don't.

So I head out of the hotel, moving a bit faster now without my suitcase, turn right and down the road towards the shopping centre. The station, I know, is at the bottom of the hill from there. But actually, looking at all the identical snow-covered streets, with identical ten foot high mountains of cleared snow on every corner, I see that the road on my left that I intended to take leads uphill, and the station is definitely at the bottom of a hill. I must have got confused. I go round the next corner and look up and down the street, but there's still nothing familiar in the white-out. To make it worse, I'm having trouble staying upright. Apart from the main thoroughfares, there has been very little gritting, and every time there's the slightest slope to the pavement I feel my feet slithering away from under me. I am very disorientated now, my hat is down over my eyes, I'm freezing despite the many layers of clothing, and it's taking all my concentration not to slip over. I skid again, have to do a bit of arm waving to regain my balance, and a woman walking past sniggers. No one skids in Helsinki. I turn another corner, lift the hat back over my eyebrows and think that this street looks very familiar. Then I realise – it *is* very familiar. I'm right in front of my hotel again. How would I survive in the forest?

Now I will have to abandon the plan to go to the station; it's got far too late and I can't risk missing soundcheck – after all, it's my first time on electric guitar and I have no idea how it will sound.

At least I know the way to the Semifinal club. Always a pleasure to walk in here: the soundman welcomes me and we set about getting a decent guitar sound. We're all done fairly quickly, and as there are still a couple of hours before stage time I decide to have one more attempt to pick up my rail tickets: I really do know the way to the station from the Semifinal – I do, I do, I do.

It's a good job I go: the confirmation number Rowan emailed me proves to be wrong so I can't get the tickets. Only one thing to do: back to the hotel to check the email – there's always an outside chance I copied it down wrongly. But no, after I've trudged back up the road, I can see on my laptop that I copied it down correctly. I text Rowan to tell him the problem and a few minutes later he sends me the number again – one digit different from the email.

So it's back down to the station – I'm getting good at this now – where I finally get the tickets and hurry back to the venue, almost late for my gig.

My friend Tommi is DJ tonight, and he's spinning some great old punk singles as I walk in. He tells me that last weekend he played his first gig with the new version of his band, who in this incarnation play exclusively Rezillos covers, translated into Finnish.

'How was it?' I ask.

'I think it was the first time in thirty years we have played a gig right,' he says, 'so I don't really know.'

Another member of the band is standing near the DJ booth, and we talk about the severe winter. He tells me that there has been so much snow that his roof is in danger of collapsing. 'In fact,' he says, 'I was supposed to be clearing the snow off my roof this evening, but I decided to come to your concert instead.'

How guilty am I going to feel if it's fallen in by the time he gets home?

I had managed to get a reasonable sound out of the guitar at soundcheck, but it doesn't last long once the gig starts. As I thrash away I find myself continually bashing the knobs and pickup switch and accidentally changing the settings. How do electric guitarists manage to hold back? After a couple of songs I have to ask the sound engineer to come up to the stage and tape over all the controls. It doesn't feel natural to be playing this guitar, but now and again on certain songs it seems to work. Slowly I find myself getting into the swing of it, and to my relief the audience are enjoying the gig. The place isn't as full as some of the times I've played here, but it's not bad for a Tuesday and the applause coming up at the end of every song sounds like a big crowd having the time of their lives.

Afterwards someone tells me: I was in a really bad mood before, and now I'm in a really good mood.

I suddenly realise: me too.

Another guy tells me he missed both my Helsinki gigs last year. Just before the first one he was rushed into hospital to have a kidney transplant. Just before the next one his doctor told him there were complications with the kidney and he had to go to back for another stay in the hospital. Earlier this year, he got a call from his doctor again and was told that he needed to go in for a check up on the ninth of February. The ninth… the ninth…that rings a bell, he thought… Oh no, it's the TV Smith gig again! He was convinced that it was a sign he'd be sent back to hospital, but to his amazement he was given the all clear and now he's here!

Outside, no one on the streets.

00:43

Minus 11 C

10th February

Harri is waiting at Tampere station to drive me to Virrat, the small town a couple of hours away where he lectures at a music college. For the second time here, the students are organising a gig for me in their local bar, Pub 66. The countryside around is a wintry wonderland and as we climb into the hills, the fir trees become heavy with thick snow, so laden that they lean down wearily over the road. Here and there, stands of silver birch can be seen, their upper branches a frosty haze of white against the powder blue sky.

'Beautiful weather,' says Harri. It's the first day it hasn't snowed for weeks: the sun is out and everywhere the snow is glittering like tinsel. It's been really cold out here in the open country, Harri tells me, and there have been some scare stories in the local papers about wolves being seen in the forests around Virrat looking for food. 'There could be some wolves,' he agrees, 'but they wouldn't attack people. Maybe they have killed a few dogs, but they would run away from people.'

Thanks for the heads up, Harri. All the same, I might cancel that stroll in the forest.

We go to the college, and I'm told that I am going to be sleeping tonight in a flat that is usually used for Bar 66 staff in the summer season but is currently empty. The only problem is, we can't get the key until six. Meanwhile I can stay the afternoon with one of the students – as soon as we can get the key to the college car so someone can drive me over there.

At the student's flat there is an internet connection so I can deal with my emails. One of them is from my brother at the workshop with a couple of photos of my guitar being repaired.

Finally the key for the accommodation is obtained, and Antte – who's been assigned the job of driving me around today – takes me out there. It's a warm, spacious flat in the forest, a couple of kilometres out of town, perfect for me even if somehow spookily far away from any signs of civilisation. I have half an hour to get settled there before Antte comes back to drive me to the venue for soundcheck.

After that, there are three interviews to do. Then I go and relax in a room upstairs and chat with the student who is going to be playing a short solo set as opener. He tells me that he usually plays in a band and recently they had a gig in the 'other' pub in Virrat, just across the road. There were only a few students from the college in, he says, the rest of the audience were old local drunks who shouted at them and told them to get a proper job.

Out of the window I can see the temperature on the digital readout on a nearby building dropping almost minute by minute…minus 16….minus 17… Good God, minus 20! On no, that's the time: 20:00.

When I go back downstairs I'm happy to see the place full of students, no old drunks – except possibly me. I start the show by mentioning that I have played San Francisco only once in my life, but now I am playing Virrat for the second time! That gets a big cheer and we're off to a good start. Still can't get used to the sound of this electric guitar, but the audience don't seem to mind and the gig is great.

Back at the flat, the fact that I haven't eaten since this morning strikes me somewhat forcibly. Antte left tomorrow's breakfast in a cool bag in the outbuilding and he told me earlier that I should bring it in before I went to bed to stop the contents freezing. In a reversal from the norm, the purpose of the cool bag is to stop things getting too cold. I go and fetch it now, the word *wolf* only crossing my mind for the briefest of instants..

So what do we have? Despite the hunger, I don't feel like the muesli, but I put some in a bowl with some milk and yoghurt to soak for a Swiss-style *bircher* muesli in the morning. Instead…hmmm, what else? Well, a bit of a change from the emergency cheese sandwich: there is no cheese, so I have some bread. Toasted!

11th February

It's not a muesli that improves with soaking – it seems to have turned to glue.

Annte picks me up and takes me over to the college where I'm handed over to Janne, who will drive me back to Tampere for my train to Pori. There is a slight delay before we can get into his car as the doors are frozen.

On the train it occurs to me that because the itinerary came so late I didn't get time to look up where the hotel or venue is so I'm not sure what I will do when I reach Pori. Luckily a very helpful lady behind the ticket desk at the station is on hand, circles where I need to go on a tourist map and points me in the right direction. The pavement down towards the hotel is a packed, ungritted layer of snow over ice. I edge along, trying to keep control of guitar, shoulder bag and suitcase, and am only yards away from my destination when inevitably – but for the first time ever in Finland – I fall over, bags and guitar skittering away from me as I slither sideways, fail to make a recovery and suddenly find myself lying on the floor. A man walking behind me looks down and mutters at me, shaking his head in disapproval. He doesn't offer to help me up. Since when has disapproval been the appropriate reaction to someone falling over?

At the reception desk they seem to know who I am even before I say. Maybe all English musicians come in limping and covered with snow all down one side of their clothes? There is an internet connection in the room so I spend some time googling the addresses of the rest of the venues and hotels for this tour. I also get another email from the guitar workshop with the latest photos of the repair. The neck is back attached to the body and it's in clamps – looking good.

I head down to the venue, just a twenty minute walk away for an Englishman – probably a Finn could cover it in ten. Little old ladies are zipping past me. The club is a lovely old cinema with a high stage and a high-end sound system. Someone is soundchecking as I walk in: a local band called Appendix, who formed only shortly after The Adverts and have a legendary status in these parts. I'll be supporting them tonight. The singer says hello and tells me how happy he is to see another old guy still out there doing it.

After soundcheck I go back to the hotel for a couple of hours. The breakfast gluesli must have finally worn off because I'm feeling hungry by the time I get there. Today's contract provides for a meal at the hotel so I order a vegetarian pizza from the restaurant there, eat half in my room, then fold the other half together and wrap it up in a napkin for after the gig. It's good to stick with tradition: after all, a cold folded pizza is actually a cheese sandwich.

I'm back at the venue an hour before my stage time of ten, but there are very few people in and we push it back half an hour. Just when I feel I can't wait any longer and have made the decision to start now no matter how small the crowd, the DJ plays 'Gary Gilmore's Eyes.' Just what every musician dreads: going on stage to 'the hit.' The guitarist from the other band gives me a sympathetic smile. 'So, what's your first number *not* going to be?'

I wait until the DJ has played another one. Even by then there are only forty people there, and they hang back from the stage and only clap politely at the end of the songs. I'm not too concerned: it's my first time here and the Finnish people take a little while before they'll tell you what they think of you. By the end of the set some are even clapping along, and although when I leave the stage and set up a little table to sell my CDs after the show almost no one comes over to me at first, just as Appendix get on stage a girl wanders over and tells me that it was the best gig she'd ever seen here, and then, under the cover of volume as the band begins, a steady trickle of people introduce themselves.

After the gig I have a couple of drinks with the band then set off back to the hotel. Outside the streets are empty and seem under some kind of magical spell: light snow floats down around me, the icy pavements twinkle in the streetlights and there is a hush over the town as if the rest of the world has been swallowed up. The only sound is the crunch of my footsteps. Enjoying the chill and the silence and the fairytale atmosphere, I decide to try a different route. This is a mistake. After some considerable time trudging along identical-looking white, snow covered streets I realise I have completely lost my bearings. Then up ahead, a glimmer of hope: the distant signs of a Hesburger burger outlet and a Subway that I definitely remember from the route to the venue. But when I get there they turn out to be different branches from the ones I saw earlier. I finally see someone walking towards me and stop her to ask the way. I can't remember the name of the hotel and my hands are too cold to get out the folder with my itinerary so I ask for the bus station, which I know is just on the other side of the square from it. She doesn't speak much in the way of English, is fairly drunk, and the directions she gives me don't quite work out the way they should, but somehow I eventually find myself in familiar territory – just around the corner from the venue. This time I take the route I know back to the hotel, and after only another twenty minutes I gratefully open the door to my warm room. I would never survive in the forest.

I drift off to sleep to the groan and clank of bulldozers moving snow about in the town square below my window,

12th February

An 8:30 alarm: I'm going to spend the afternoon doing some recording near Tampere with Japi from a band called King Of All The Animals so need an early start. I grab a quick breakfast, then pack my things hurriedly and set off for the station. The temperature is a heady minus five and by the time I get there I've broken out in a light sweat.

Japi picks me up from Tampere station and drives me out to his studio in a small town half an hour away. There we have an excellent afternoon recording vocals and guitar on a couple of songs for a musical project he's working on. It goes so smoothly and I'm so happy with the results that I transfer some demos I've recorded for my next album from my laptop onto his equipment and sing some vocals for those too.

Then it's back to Tampere on the train. From the station I only have a short walk to my hotel: one of the extremely practical Omena chain which drive down prices by providing no staff. You are given two code numbers: one to get in and out of all the various doors in the building, and another to get into your room. Luckily it works better than Trainline.

A new venue for me, The Dog's Home, is just on the other side of the station, not far from my two usual venues Tulliklubbi and Telakka. Recently the owners decided to start putting on bands on a free-entry basis. Rowan from Harri's agency is there to meet me when I walk in – he'll be mixing the sound tonight. He shows me the little office that I can use as a dressing room and gives me a key to the padlock on the door so I can keep my things secure there, then I set up on stage. To my surprise, when he gets to work on the Telecaster, it actually starts sounding pretty good and I find myself looking forward to the gig.

But things are never that simple. By gig time the place is fairly full. There are lots of my friends there: Jukka, Tiina from Punk Lurex, Teemu – the student who managed my tour last year – but there is something missing. Electricity. Something somewhere has fused, and now the entire PA system and stage lights are no longer working. Rowan is running around trying to figure out what is going on. 'Don't worry,' he says, clearly worried himself, 'an electrician will be here in fifteen minutes! It's the guy who wired up the place!'

I wander over to the bar. Tiina is there and tells me there are people fiddling about with fuse boxes down the corridor by the toilets. I speculate that maybe they are going to use the electricity from the toilets to power the stage. Actually, maybe they really are – I'd better use the loo while there's still light in there.

In the Gents I find Jukka in front of me in the queue. I say to him, 'Smashed guitar, no sound, no lights – it's all going very well!'

He grins. 'There is one very good thing about this situation. You will have another chapter for your diary.'

I say, 'Right now that is about the only thing that is keeping me hanging on.'

I go back to the dressing room but can't make the key open the padlock so stand outside the door feeling like a fool. I grab Rowan as he dashes past. 'This is probably not your biggest problem right now,' I say, 'but I can't make this work. Is it me or is it broken?'

He grabs the key from my hand. *Snick-snack.* The door opens. 'It's you,' he says, and hurries off back towards the stage.

I strap on my guitar in the dressing room and play though a few things, trying to get used to the feel of the Telecaster, worried about whether the gig is going to happen. Normally I would know that in the extreme worst case scenario I could use the acoustic guitar and do the gig without any power at all but of course today that's not possible.

Rowan puts his head round the door. 'We have the sound system up and running,' he says. 'The lights aren't working but we're going to rewire them so there's at least one spot on you. Going to be five minutes and then we start.'

By the time five minutes is up it's nearly 11:30, half an hour after my advertised start time, and the place is full to bursting. People are crowded up in front of the stage and it turns into a great gig.

Afterwards I hang around having a drink with some of the audience. One guy catches me at the bar and offers to buy me a beer. In halting English he says, 'I only caught the last half hour, but I thought you really had a lot of…er…er…'

'Energy?' I suggest.

'No…er…you really had a lot of the sound of the revival of the New Wave of British Heavy Metal.'

Aha. I'm grabbed by another group of people, one guy and a couple of girls. 'We want two photos,' the guy says, 'One normal, and one making a stupid face.'

I get a stupid face ready, then just as the shutter is about to click he suddenly inserts his finger up my nose. I can tell you, it was an even stupider face than the one I'd planned.

Omena hotels. Brilliant concept until you come back at 2:15 and two Finnish women arrive just before you. They punch in their code and hold the door open for you because they are too polite to insist that you punch in your own code. You trail behind them down a short corridor, then the same thing happens at the next door. Then you wait for the lift together, which takes some time because there are five floors. I'm on the fifth, which is unfortunate, because so are they, and they've already pressed the '5' button after I follow them in, and when I stand there with them all the way up, I can see them getting distinctly restless – surely if I was a genuine guest it would be just too much of a coincidence to be on the same floor? When we get out of the lift, the one who knows the codes makes a half-hearted attempt to hold back before walking over to the code box, but in the millisecond where I could have stepped forward to put *my* code in, she has become too self conscious to go through with the artifice and has walked forward and started entering her code, with the inevitable result that I follow them through this door too, and down the corridor afterwards. As luck would have it, they turn left at the end and I turn right. They hesitate outside their door, glancing surreptitiously in my direction, and when I punch in my room code and the lock clicks open, the sense of relief in the corridor is palpable.

13th February

My train for Seinäjoke doesn't leave until mid-afternoon so I get the chance to catch up on some sleep. No worries about missing breakfast – the Omena doesn't do one anyway, but Teemu is running an all-day breakfast club at the Tulliklubbi and has invited me along. There's a relaxed atmosphere there, a buffet laid out and some soft music playing gently in the background. I have to interrupt the owner of the place as he enthusiastically tells me that I have just got to try the local black sausage speciality… but there is also a tofu sausage version. It's great to spend a couple of hours relaxing, getting some good food and coffee down, and still have time to change strings and get myself set up for the gig this evening. Just before I leave for my train, Rowan arrives and tells me yesterday was a full house and people were waiting outside in the sub-zero temperatures in the hope someone else would leave and they would be allowed in.

I'm looking forward to tonight's gig too: I've played the Bar 15 in Seinäjoke before, and it was a really good one. I have left myself half an hour to cover the 100 metres to the station but it still may not be enough. The road down there is at quite a gradient and hasn't been gritted to any useful extent so I have to inch along the pavement, pawing at anything solid I can find as I make my uncertain way. I develop the technique of using my roller suitcase like a kind of lateral Zimmer frame, and as soon as I start to feel my feet slipping out from under me I yank the case sideways so the wheels dig in and hang on for dear life. I seriously consider straddling the handle and gliding the rest of the way on what would be the world's first luggage-based toboggan.

On the train, sitting in my individual pool of water, I wonder if it can be true, what someone told me the first time I came here: that Doctor Martens freeze over. It occurs to me that when I first come out of the hotel each morning, my shoes warm from a night next to the radiator, I can walk along fairly effortlessly but the more the day wears on the more slippy they seem to get.

In Seinäjoke the hotel is right opposite the station, so I can drop my suitcase right off there, then it's just a short clomp down the road to the club. I've just found out clomping helps, even if it makes you look like a robot. I tell the club owner at Bar 15 about my problems walking and he tells me about a friend of his who is a teacher and recently took a class of kids up to Lapland. Their hosts gave him a pair of snow shoes and he set up the class for a group photo wearing them, but by the time he got back to the camera he was finding them so cumbersome he took them off again. He told the kids to hold their position and walked back towards the group intending to adjust the way one of them was standing. Halfway there he suddenly dropped through the snow up to his chest.

At soundcheck we spend some time working on the guitar sound and eventually I'm happy with it. The trick seems to be, turn the treble all the way down. The gig goes like a dream. Usually, this is a tables and chairs venue but right from the first note the crowd are up on their feet and in front of the stage singing along and punching the air. 'Did you *feel* the atmosphere in the room?!' the owner asks me afterwards.

I did feel it. I felt it all over Finland over the last five days.

Back at the hotel, I quickly check my emails before bed. There's one from my brother, showing the guitar back in one piece again, ready for delivery the day after tomorrow just in time for my unplugged fully-acoustic gig in London. It's been an interesting experience, playing electric. Over the last couple of days I've finally been getting used to the technique and finding how to get the most out of it and which songs work best. I may even try using it now and again in the future. But the broken acoustic seemed symptomatic of all the problems I'd been struggling against to keep on gigging recently; the fact that it is now mended is surely a sign that I am back on the heavily-gritted road to recovery, and right now I can't wait to return to what I'm used to, put the problems behind me and get my feet back on solid ground. You never get used to slippy.

Guitar break

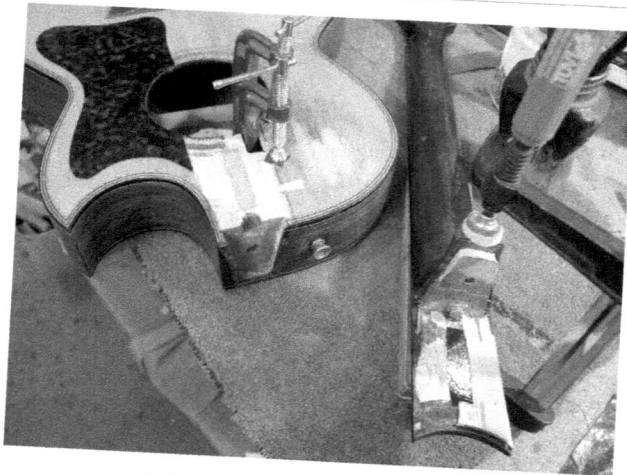

We can rebuild it

8. HAWAIIGOLAND (2010)

<u>29th April</u>

I'm off to Heligoland, for a weekend festival called the *Rock'n'Roll Butterfahrt*, organised by a guy called Tim who a while ago promoted a gig for me in his home town of Wilhelmshaven. The festival is co-organised by a German punk band called The Mimmis, who play it every year.

Last year's festival in September would have been the fourth, but was abandoned when bad weather meant all the ferries were cancelled so no one could get there. They moved it to May this year hoping for better weather and are now calling it *Rock'n'Roll Butterfahrt 4.1*. Their bad luck was my good luck — I wasn't actually booked for the original, but have been added to the bill for the re-scheduled version.

Heligoland! Most people don't know where it is. When I told my friend Australian stand-up comedian Bruce Griffiths why I couldn't meet him when he visits London tomorrow he said, 'Heligoland? Is that near Legoland?'

It's an island up off the coast of Northern Germany and Denmark. Just getting there is a trial: the crossing takes two and a half hours and then the ferries can't get in close to the island so everyone has to take their luggage and transfer to small open-top motor boats. There's no way I could do the trip in one day, so tonight a gig has been arranged for me in a town called Rendsburg, just an hour away from where the ferry leaves early tomorrow morning.

I fly in to Hamburg and am met by Finn and Meike, who Tim told me would be there to pick me up. I know it's them because one of them is wearing a TV Smith T-shirt. Rendsburg is their home town and they are organising the gig in a Greek restaurant there called the Akropolis. We have time to kill before soundcheck so divert off the motorway and cross the canal to Rendsburg on its major tourist attraction — an old hanging ferry suspended on cables from the railway bridge overhead. The metal platform has just enough space for four cars and a few bicycles and pedestrians, and is one of only five in the world. Only three of them are still in working condition, but that's not bad after 100 years. If only the engineer who built it could have known! He was so nervous about whether it would work or not that the day before it opened he committed suicide.

The only other tourist attraction is on the opposite bank, the *Schiffsbegrußungsanlage*, which roughly translates as a man in a glass booth announcing the name and destination of the passing ships. Loudspeakers outside a restaurant play a burst of stirring music for each one, the ships sound their klaxons and everyone on the restaurant terrace waves. The weather is warm so we sit at a table with a beer and enjoy the show. I find myself getting quite excited when a brand new ship, blue paint still gleaming, glides past pulled by two tugs. It's not finished yet, announces the DJ. It's going to Hamburg to get its engines fitted out! Toot toot!

We drive on to the Greek Restaurant and Finn explains the plans for the rest of the day and tomorrow. After soundcheck he'll take me over to my hotel, which is just a few hundred metres away. I'll need to be back here by eight – the gig will start early because much of the audience will, like us, have to wake up early to catch the ferry from Bösum. Then when we get to Heligoland, he'll 'hand me over' to Tim. I don't know if I've ever been handed over before. Tim and some of the rest of the team arrived in Heligoland yesterday, Finn explains, to start building the stage on the beach.

Just a minute. On the beach? *Outside?* An open-air gig on an island in the middle of the North Sea in April? Somehow I thought it would be in a club. Now I learn from Finn that it's not even the main island – Heligoland consists of two: the thriving port and tourist centre, bustling with restaurants and duty-free shops; then there's the other one, the dune island, which is – er – just dunes, a shop and restaurant, a landing strip for light aircraft, and a handful of wooden holiday bungalows. At least I'll be staying in one of those, unlike most of the audience who will be camping. Let's hope the sun keeps shining.

The owner of the restaurant comes out to greet us. After chatting for a couple of minutes he excuses himself: 'I've got to go back to the kitchen now. I've just had a delivery of 140 kilos of meat and I have to prepare it.'

Hmm, wonder what I'll get to eat tonight. Or over the weekend, come to that. After soundcheck I go to the supermarket opposite the hotel and buy some rye bread (keeps longer than ordinary bread) and a vacuum pack of cheese. The emergency cheese sandwich is coming to Heligoland!

I'm back at the restaurant half an hour before gig time. Not too many people have arrived yet. I am beginning to wonder if it might have been a bit optimistic putting on a gig here, but Finn tells me that he's heard from quite a few who are still on the way. There's two coming from Belgium, for example, and then some I know from my Düsseldorf gigs, Nina and Chappo among them. Finn takes a phone call. 'They're on the way over now,' he tells me, then listens again. 'They're in the same hotel as you!'

Quite handy, because it means Finn won't have to pick me up in the morning – instead Nina and Chappo can drive me and we'll save some time.

Against my expectations, pretty soon the restaurant is full, and so I start my set. There is no stage, I play at one end of the room against a background of large plant pots, alabaster statues and bunches of plastic grapes. It's a practical spot to play, because as round after round of *Jägermeister* and Ouzo get handed to me I am able to take a tiny polite sip and then hide the nearly-full glasses behind the giant plant pots, thus avoiding being blind drunk by the time I get to the end of my ninety minute-plus set.

After I've finished things eventually quieten down in the restaurant and the owners bring me out a large plate of vegetarian food. I sit at a table next to Chappo, who is just finishing off a meal. 'Unbelievable,' he says. 'When they found out we'd come all the way from Düsseldorf they gave us the food for free!'

It's going to be a 6:30 start tomorrow morning so now it's time to pack up and head back to the hotel. Before I go, the boss of the restaurant presents me with a bottle of ouzo, which I don't really want because I'm trying to travel light, but accept out of politeness. Of course, they might not think I'm so polite when they clean up tomorrow and find the stash of drinks behind the plant pot.

30th April

6:30 a.m. and outside the skies are leaden and it's pouring with rain. Nina and friends are already in the breakfast room when I get there. 'Nice day!' I say, as I head for the buffet.

Nina gestures at the window, 'Northern Germany sunshine.'

I'm just pouring the muesli into the bowl when I hear a crash behind me and see Nina crumpling to the floor. At first I think she's tripped up, but in fact she has fainted. Maybe too many ouzos last night. Chappo hurries over and cradles her head as she lies on the floor looking confused. He escorts her back to the bedroom, and she faints again on the way. We're now running late to meet Finn, who's going to lead a convoy of cars to the ferry. As there is only one ferry a day, if we miss that we'll miss the festival.

Ten minutes later Chappo is back. 'She's laughing. That's a good sign.'

She's also refusing to go to hospital, so it looks like the *Rock 'n' Roll Butterfahrt* is back on.

Happily, Nina stays conscious throughout the journey, though a little green in the face as we speed Northwards. With ten minutes to spare we pull into the car park by the docks where the ferry 'Funny Lady' is waiting for us. Rain-soaked bedraggled groups of punks, including many familiar faces that I've seen at my gigs, are unloading bags and tents from their cars. Nina rushes off towards the toilets.

On board I'm delighted to see Vom's friends Micha and Uli, who lent us their brand new van for our tour last year. They'll be staying in one of the bungalows near me with some other friends of ours, Mel and Pinky and their new baby. We stash our bags and my guitar on the upper deck, then stake our place at a few tables downstairs. Through the portholes the sea is a grim grey expanse. Soon the first beers are being opened.

Nina has a lot more colour in her face now and is even contemplating drinking one herself. 'I've had breakfast twice,' she says, 'once going in, once coming back out.'

Through the misty rain, Heligoland and its neighbouring dune island slowly appear. The ferry stops its engines and all the passengers transfer into the smaller boats which speed us bumpily over to the landing ramp, where the rest of the festival crew are waiting to greet us. There is a banner reading 'Welcome to Hawaiigoland,' and a man dressed in a sea captain's uniform hands out gaily coloured plastic garlands to us all as we step onto dry land. For the hardier souls there are shots of rum. Someone is playing a trumpet.

Tim hands me the key to my bungalow, which I'll be sharing with the Mimmis. They should be arriving, along with most of the rest of the expected 400 audience, on the ferry out of Cuxhaven which arrives in half an hour. I don't feel like hanging around out here in the chilly wind to wait for them so I carry my guitar and bags over to the bungalows to warm up.

There are twenty-five gaily-painted wooden holiday bungalows, separated from each other by banks of grassy sand about a metre high. A couple of women from the company who rent the bungalows out – usually to regular nature-loving tourists – are leading a party of punk rockers ahead of me and I tag along behind. My bungalow is the first one you come to, so rather than go to the far end and follow the maze of paths back to it, I hoist my guitar and suitcase over the bank and scramble over. As I do I hear angry shouts from the women. These man-made banks are part of the *Dünenschutz*, the environmental protection measures to preserve the island, they tell me, and in no uncertain terms they make it known that I have committed a crime comparable with scuppering an oil tanker on a coral reef.

The bungalow is a much more civilised affair than I had expected: newly renovated with kitchen area, heating, oven, bathroom and shower; it really is quite comfortable. I put my guitar and bag in one of the bedrooms then go back out to the harbour to meet the next arrivals. The Cuxhaven ferry is a good deal bigger than ours and soon the jetty is swarming with people, the Mimmis among them. 'Isn't this great?' says their singer Fabsi, gesturing at the crowd, who are all happy and smiling despite the cold. There's a real sense of excitement in the air. I walk with the band back towards our bungalow but on the way stop by the neighbouring one, which has been set up as the festival office, because I need to have a chat with Tim about arrangements for the weekend. There are still a few details to be cleared up: for example, where is the stage, when is soundcheck, what time do I play, how do I get to Hamburg on Sunday when I get back to the mainland, and where do I sleep when I get there? Just details.

Tim admits he has been too busy to sort things out for me, but there is a computer in the office with a very slow internet connection and he promises he'll get round to it. The other question is what to do about food, but he tells me there will be something for the musicians available at the festival site. 'You're not vegetarian are you? Ah…you are. Mmm, well, there will be – um – I think, some minestrone.'

Not usually vegetarian. So I march off to the airstrip café, quite a lengthy hike, and buy the one vegetarian item I can find – a can of *ohne fleisch* ratatouille. Doesn't look too appetising, but it will do if I can't find anything else, and I still have the cheese and bread from Rendsburg for an emergency cheese sandwich if necessary.

The sound guy is supposed to turn up at five, so I leave it until 5:30 until I head over to the stage. I'm opening the festival so I hope there'll be time for a quick soundcheck to make sure everything's working before I start. Although only a few hundred metres past the bungalows I have to make quite a detour before I find the stage as all ways seem to be blocked by the *Dünenschutz* and it's well past six by the time I find it, down a path near the dune café. There's nothing happening though, so after a while, bored of watching the soundman plugging in cables, I go for a wander up the beach, surprising myself when an outcrop of rocks I head towards turns out to be a shoal of seals basking on the edge of the sea. Unlike me, they are blissfully unaware of the arctic wind blasting in from the North.

Sunbathing here takes a hardy spirit, and deckchairs on Heligoland are solid wooden boxes with a padded bench inside, like a one-man beach hut. I settle in one of those when I get back to the festival area as there is still nothing happening. Tim is digging a hole to plant a pirate flag.

At eight Fabsi goes on stage to introduce me and I get a big cheer as I follow him up, plug in the guitar, say hello and launch into the opening song. From up here I can look over the heads of the audience and see the silvery strip of sand and the wide expanse of grey sea all the way up to the horizon, where there is a final burst of light as the sun flares between two jagged clouds. The only disturbing thing is the stiff chilly wind blowing into my face and up the arms of my T-shirt. It's the first time I can recall feeling cold on stage. I try and ignore the temperature, helped by the sight of the dancers kicking up the sand in front of me. Everything is going marvellously, but then right in the middle of Gary Gilmore's Eyes all the power goes off. A groan goes up from the crowd and I step up to the edge of the stage and carry on acoustically. The wind whips most of the sound away, but people gather round as close as they can get and attempt to sing and clap along to the little they can hear. There's a huge cheer at the end so I carry straight on with Bored Teenagers. Halfway through that the sound comes on again, I finish off with One Chord Wonders and leave the stage with the feeling that the things that went wrong made the show even better.

Afterwards I put on another T-shirt and a jacket over what I'm already wearing and walk over to the bar. Tim tells me we were lucky: last year the power went off on the entire island for quite a few hours. No one was even allowed to use the toilets because the sewage system also went out of action.

Someone says to me, 'That was amazing! And I heard you just flew in from a gig yesterday in Greece for this festival!'

Slight misunderstanding there.

Surprisingly Nina is still buzzing around and bursting with energy, clearly unaffected by her breakfast collapse. 'I am getting married tomorrow on stage to my friend Anneliese,' she announces. 'Fabsi is going to be the priest and Chappo will be Best Man. TV, will you come on stage and present the rings?'

I'm not sure that I'm qualified, but I say yes. I don't have a gig tomorrow – any excuse to get on stage.

The final band of the evening begins – a duo from Hamburg called Jonny Glut, who play folky songs with a sea shanty feel. I'm now so cold I don't know if I'm enjoying the band or not, but my friend Lio has no such doubts. Not a fan of folk music, I see her grimace as another accordion passage starts, and she says, 'Lets go back to my bungalow and have a drink.'

I explain that I've lent Jonny Glut my guitar cable and if I leave now I'll never see it again – that's the law if you ever lend out your guitar cable – so we shiver through another couple of numbers and then I say, 'Fuck the cable, let's go.'

It turns out that Lio is in one of the older bungalows near the landing strip, quite a distance away from mine. It's only when we have left the lights of the festival area behind us that we suddenly become aware that we are on a very dark unpopulated island. Lio looks in the direction of where she thinks the bungalows are and hesitantly sets off down one of the two dark paths snaking off into the dunes. There is a dimly-lit building ahead that must surely be something to do with the airfield, but the closer we get the more uncertain of our orientation we become. Can it be that we're on the wrong side of the landing strip? There is no one about, no other landmarks, just the low black silhouettes of the dunes, and all we can hear is the distant crashing of the waves and the sound of Jonny Glut, who is still playing despite having started on what seemed like his closing song, with the repeated chorus *Bye Bye, Bye Bye* as we were leaving.

Eventually we lose our nerve. 'It must have been the other path,' says Lio, and we turn back. We're almost at the festival again when we meet a few people who assure us that we were going the right way, so we turn around and retrace our steps. Sure enough, past the airport building, there's the shop – it's all making sense. With relief we tumble into the bungalow where a few of Lio's friends are sitting cosily around in the comparative warmth.

It's even more of a relief to put my guitar and bag down and open a beer. Over the dunes we hear the sound of applause as the band finally finishes. The live music has to end comparatively early because some of the audience need to get the last ferry at midnight over to Heligoland as there weren't enough camping places for everyone on the dune island. There will be a DJ set from Fabsi for a few hours yet for those who are staying.

These old bungalows are nice enough – apart from the fact they don't have their own bathrooms so you have to share the communal facilities just up the path – but soon I'm keen to get back to my place. There's only one problem: I have to find it.

Yes – somewhere out there, far away across the other side of the dunes is home. I head off in what I think might be the right direction, assuring all the worried people in Lio's bungalow that I'll be fine. I'll just head off more or less in the direction of the main island over there across the channel, easy to follow thanks to the lighthouse on the cliffs above it. And, yes, I came down this path earlier today when I went to the shop – I recognise the little outcrops of tents nestled in among the dunes, out of the worst of the wind. But goodness, in the darkness…there are paths leading off paths… twisting back on themselves, thinning out to dead ends…

I come across a very drunk punk rocker standing forlornly and swaying a little. 'Please,' he wails, 'where is the camping place? I am lost!' He looks like he might burst into tears.

'I'm lost too,' I explain, 'but I did just see the some tents back down there.'

He thinks about it. 'I'm following you,' he decides.

'I'm not going to the camping place! You need to go back that way!'

He staggers gamely after me for a few paces before giving up.

As I approach the other side of the island the wind suddenly drops and a hush falls. There is darkness all around except for the broad beam of the lighthouse which sweeps at regular intervals across the bay. In its intermittent light I recognise the narrow concrete path I am heading down as the one that leads to the ferry jetty, only two minutes from my bungalow. And then, there it is, just on the other side of that low dune bank, home sweet home.

It's the middle of the night, I've had a few drinks, the place is deserted. Do I go all the way round the path? Do I fuck.

1st May

I was kind of surprised to find the place empty when I got back last night, but then I realised it was actually only about one in the morning. Which did mean that I could settle myself in my room and get my head down undisturbed and wake up feeling reasonably fresh. I come out of the bedroom to find the bungalow is full of people, the other bedroom door shut, two bodies on the fold-out double bed in the living room, another on a sleeping mat laid out in the kitchen area with a bucket next to it. We all know what a bucket next to the bed means and I don't investigate any further. All is peaceful apart from the odd gentle snore. I tiptoe into the shower and when I emerge, Fabsi – for it is he – is rousing from the living room bed and announcing his intention to go over to the airstrip café where they have a buffet breakfast. I join him.

The café is full, the yoghurt bowl is empty, and the vegetarian option is pretty much bread and cheese but there's fruit juice and coffee, and it's nice sitting at a table with Fabsi and a few fans from Düsseldorf. Jonny Glut comes over and tells me he was blown away by my set. (I was almost literally blown away.) Even better: he remembered the cable and has dropped it off in my bungalow.

The big daytime event is the Pirate Challenge, where a few brave souls, still suffering from last night's excesses, take part in five team events, most of them involving alcohol. Earlier, on my way to breakfast, when I saw Finn outside his bungalow already chugging back a beer he told me it was 'training.'

I arrive at the festival area just as the first round is about to take place. This one actually doesn't involve any drinking at all, you just have to run as fast as you can along a short course in front of the stage with a beer crate full of sand on your shoulder. With soft sand beneath your feet and a body weakened by last night's excesses it's more difficult than you might think, and I have to wince as one of Finn's team almost immediately trips up and sprawls onto the floor, the case hitting him in the throat and leaving a nasty bruise.

The next game involves the teams digging up cans of beer that Tim has buried in the sand and drinking them as fast as possible. Apart from the fact the cans are hidden in the sand, this is not much different from what the contestants do most of the day anyway.

The next rounds are more grisly. In the tented area at the back by the bar there is a task which involves eating cooked seaweed against the clock, and ends with a number of contestants running out of the tent towards the beach, cheeks bulging. I have a sniff of one of the bowls and it's almost enough to make me throw up without even tasting it. Then there's the game where six shot glasses are lined up. Three are bourbon, three are whale liver oil, and you have to drink them as fast as possible. Damn, if only

I wasn't vegetarian I could be in one of the teams too, but the whale liver oil means I simply can't. Oh well.

It's still only early afternoon, and Micha and Uli – who've been watching the Pirate Challenge with me – ask if I feel like taking the ferry over to Heligoland with them and Mel and Pinky. Sounds like a good plan, so we go back to our bungalows and arrange to meet up when the next ferry leaves in half an hour. Coincidentally I get a text from Lio, saying she's going there too, and the two Belgians turn out to be on the same ferry so the gang's all here!

Before attempting the walk up to the cliffs to see the only tourist attraction in Heligoland – a big cliff set slightly apart from the other big cliffs – we divert into a restaurant to build up our strength. The only vegetarian dish on offer is a 'Vegetarian Surprise.' I don't like surprises so I order the asparagus instead, which also surprises me as somewhere in its preparation it has undergone a complete taste bypass.

After eating we tramp up the towering flight of steps to the cliff tops. The weather has closed in so there's not a lot to see up there apart from a few birds and we plod around the paths getting increasingly damp in the misty rain. We walk past the crater where the biggest conventional bomb ever – 500 kilos – was dropped by the English in the war. We've almost done the complete circuit of the island now, and we realise that it's got quite late and if we're going to get back in time for tonight's bands we should leave for the ferry.

Back in my bungalow on the dune island, the Mimmis are packing their gear ready to head over to the stage for their gig tonight. I follow them shortly afterwards but first I put on every T-shirt I've brought with me (4) under my jacket.

It's ridiculous: from the top of the path to the stage I can actually see the roof of Lio's bungalow across the dunes. How could we possibly have got so lost? All today I have been imagining how the place looks in the dark to make sure it doesn't happen again tonight.

A girl waves at me as I go past. 'TV! I am Annaliese, Nina's husband-to-be!'

Nina soon finds me too and ushers me to the area behind the stage where she has everything required for the ceremony. Chappo and I join forces to get the zip done up on Nina's ambitiously tailored purple wedding dress while Anneliese gets into her gold-sprayed knee-length boots. The happy couple are both so nervous that they have rush off and pee, which results in a good telling off by Fabsi when he arrives as he's responsible for making sure people keep to the *Dünenschutz*, and running up over the high dune behind the stage where everyone can see you is rather a blatant contravention.

Then the preparations for the service continue. Fabsi gets into a priest costume, and then between bands we all troop up onto the stage. Everything goes well, I hand over the rings, rice is thrown.

I am disappointed to notice that twenty minutes after the ceremony, while the Mimmis play, Nina is cuddling up to some bloke who was drinking with us in Lio's caravan last night.

The four T-shirts aren't working. The last band to play this evening have only just started their soundcheck and already I'm thinking of sneaking back into the warm. I know Lio is dreading another Jonny Glut type experience and when someone on stage says, 'Can I have some more penny whistle in the monitors?' I hear her say, *oh nein!*

Micha is also looking cold so I suggest a trip back to Lio's bungalow might be a good idea. The snag is, the alcohol is locked in the neighbouring bungalow and Lio doesn't have the key. 'I have a bottle of ouzo in mine!' I say, and the deal is done.

I have studied the route back so carefully I could now walk it blindfolded, although Micha seems doubtful about it as the lights peter out and we appear to all intents and purposes to be in the middle of nowhere. But soon we emerge from the dark wilderness to the familiar, cosy huddle of bungalows.

Possibly too cosy. After we've warmed up and finished off the ouzo, Lio and Micha are keen to get back to the stage but I'm simply too comfortable and decide to stick where I am.

2nd May

First in bed and first awake. All are slumbering around me when I get up, but Micha invited me over to his bungalow to breakfast this morning so I wander over to see if they're up yet. The sun is shining and the wind has completely dropped. Suddenly it's Spring! On the way I see Tim outside the office and he admits that he hasn't yet figured out how I'm getting to Hamburg tonight or where I'm going to stay but he'll get it sorted this morning.

Over at Bungalow 21 they're all awake, coffee is brewing, and Micha is out fetching some things for breakfast from the shop. When he returns there are quite a lot of meaty items in his bag so I pop back to my bungalow to fetch the emergency Rendsburg cheese and bulk up the vegetarian element a bit.

The weather is so glorious that we decide to lay the table outside on the decked terrace, and we have a lazy breakfast out there, lapping up the sun. It's already past ten, officially check-out time, and two women from the rental team are wandering around trying to get everyone out. It can only be a matter of time before they start hassling us too. But when they come over, they are very friendly and say we can take our time, they'll just take the bedding now and clean up the rest later. Uli asks one of them to take a photo of the whole group, and just as she's preparing to take the shot, the other lady rushes over and unexpectedly sits on my lap. 'Might as well join in!' she laughs. Suddenly I recognise her as the person who told me off when I scrambled over the dune to my bungalow on the first day here.

The Belgians pass by just as we're discussing plans to go and have a look at the seals before we catch the ferry and they decide to come along too. Uli mentions that I have to get to Hamburg and they say they'll be driving there on their way home and can give me a lift.

I go to tell Tim that the problem of how I'm going to get to Hamburg has been solved and he tells me he has been on the laptop and found a reasonably cheap hotel 600 metres from Hamburg airport so I'll be well placed for my flight tomorrow. I leave my bags with him in the office and go to the neighbouring bungalow to say goodbye to Finn. He is sitting outside with his leg propped up, one foot in bandages and a pair of crutches beside him. He is one of many who have caught their feet in holes in the sand over the weekend. He shrugs and smiles: 'When old men try and party...'

Back to the other bungalow, where they've just finished packing all their things. Uli hands me back the pack of cheese. 'We didn't use it, so you might as well take it,' she says.

As the sun is still beating down I tell her to leave it in the fridge and I'll pick it up on the way back.

When we get back from our seal-watching, the bungalow has been locked by the cleaning crew but I really don't care. Consider the emergency cheese my little present from Rendsburg to Heligoland. And anyway I still have that bloody can of ravioli in my bag.

Hours later when I get to Hamburg there is obviously no can opener or cooker in my hotel room so it looks like the ravioli will be coming back to England with me. The guy at Reception recommends a restaurant nearby though and as I haven't eaten any hot food all weekend I decide to go for a solitary meal. I get there to find it's a Greek restaurant, which tops and tails this little tour nicely. It's also apt because the brief burst of sun this morning has left my face impressively sunburnt so I look like a tourist. None of the Greek food is vegetarian, but they do offer a veggie pizza. 'A glass of ouzo on the house?' asks the waiter.

Is there an ouzo glut this year?

'No thanks.'

He brings it anyway. And there are no plant pots nearby so I drink it.

How to get to Heligoland...

big boat...

small boat...

big welcome!

Q. When is a stage not a stage
A. When it's a wind tunnel

Off to see the sights of
Heligoland...

and there they are

The locals love it

Traditional Heligoland
wedding outfit

Blatant contravention of
the Dünenschutz

When old men party

Not rocks. Seals

9. OLD PUNKS (2010)

13th August

An early start to fly off to a punk festival featuring The Vibrators, The Lurkers, Sham 69, Texas Terri Bomb and a few others – many of the same bunch who were at the massive Rebellion punk festival in Blackpool last weekend. Now we're all going to be meeting up again in the Czech Republic. Or rather, *they* will be: I'm the only UK artist playing today, the rest are all on tomorrow. And my name isn't on the flyer.

No need to queue at the desk as I've checked in online and I'm just travelling with hand luggage; I'm only going for one night and haven't bought many CDs because I never sell much in the Czech Republic anyway. The twenty or so I have with me fit into the shoulder bag, along with a couple of tour diary books that Texas Terri asked me to bring her, and an emergency sandwich.

So it's straight through security, then a nice welcome from the girl at the coffee bar, where I'm now quite a regular visitor. I'm sitting there enjoying the caffeine starting to filter through my morning-befuddled brain when one of the airport staff arrives in front of me. 'TV Smith! Where are you off to now? Remember me, I chatted with you outside the toilets a couple of months ago.' I'm at Heathrow so often I think they should adopt me for a mascot. We talk about punk for a while, then he hurries off. 'Better go. I'm supposed to be on screening!'

There's a fifteen minute delay before boarding because they are 'waiting for a crew member,' then we miss our take-off slot and have to sit on the plane a long time before we move off. I'm pretty hungry by the time we're in the air but I'm not breaking into the emergency sandwich yet. The BA snacks seem to shrink with every flight though: this time there's the choice of a mini bag of crisps or a mini chocolate biscuit. I ask for a coffee, and the stewardess demands, 'Crisps or biscuit!'

'Biscuit,' I reply meekly. I have said it in a small child's voice.

My Czech promoter Petr is anxiously waiting at Prague airport. 'Ha, British Airways!' he exclaims. 'Expensive ticket, still delay, expect Ryanair bullshit, but BA – no tell nothing wait!'

I often wonder how much better we would get on if either of us could successfully speak each others language. His English is patchy at best, and after several visits here the only Czech words I've learned are 'beer' and 'thank you.'

'We're not going to be late are we?' I ask. 'I didn't think I was on until after nine?' It's around four now and the festival is only a fifty kilometre drive.

'No late but bullshit parking,' says Petr.

We hurry outside and I start to head for the car park, thinking of the mounting cost of his ticket, but his van, a battered converted German *Polizei* minibus, is right in front of us, parked at an eccentric angle in the yellow-lined section at the edge of a bus stop.

We speed off, first on the motorway and then down badly-maintained bumpy country lanes to the small town of Zbiroh, where the unfortunately-titled 'Old Punks Festival' is taking place. The plan is to drop in there and pick up passes, then go and check in to the hotel.

After a few wrong turns and a number of exotic Czech swear words from Petr we end up at the festival, which is set in a large field below a hill topped by an imposing baroque castle. At one end of the field a wide stage is being rigged out for the bands who will play tomorrow. Today, the electric bands play a large indoor room at the other end of the field, and the acoustic bands – me included – play in a marquee up a slope towards the castle. I can see about twenty people up there at the moment, sitting on long wooden benches at the back of the tent by the bar. I notice from the running order that I'm on at the same time that popular Czech band SPS play in the indoor room. Already I have the feeling that this is going to be a bit of a disaster.

We sit in the van for a few minutes while the heavens open and people scurry back to their tents to avoid a soaking. One scrawny white guy with long dreadlocks and dishevelled clothing who has been lying in the grass since we arrived, a half-empty plastic bottle of dubious content by his side, remains oblivious to the downpour. When the alcohol wears off he is going to wake up very wet.

When the rain dies down we go to pick up our passes from the office, and Petr finds out that he and I are staying in different hotels. They're about 30 kilometres apart so we abandon the idea of going back there before the show and instead make use of the drinks tickets and get a beer. Texas Terri will be in the same hotel as me though and we have arranged to meet at breakfast so I can give her the books. She and her band are driving down from Berlin tonight.

We are soon joined by Martin, the T-shirt maker and merchandiser for an old Czech band called Brutus, who I've played with a couple of times. He was at Rebellion last week, congratulates me on my show there and tells me he's heard nothing but good feedback about it. As for this festival here in Zbiroh, it's the first year they've held it and there are a few wrinkles still to be ironed out: he points out the packed camping area on the other side of the beer stands and explains that it needs to be extended as people are arriving all the time and there's no more room for them. The camping area has to be fenced around to stop people getting in without a ticket but the organisers have run out of fencing. 'They have some more fences coming, but for now they don't know what to do.'

Petr peruses the food stands to see if there is anything veggie for me. There's an awful lot of meat, but the little caravan on the end claims to serve Puris. The guy inside is pressing out a wad of greasy dough onto a hotplate. 'You know Govinda's in London?' he says. 'This is just like that.'

It isn't.

Petr wanders off to distribute some CDs from a band he is managing around the merchandising stands and I go to check out the acoustic stage. There is a singer/songwriter half-heartedly performing for an audience of three people, plus the soaked dreadlocks guy who has not only revived but is crazy-dancing around the tent and jumping up on the metal safety fence in front of the stage and shaking it. The stockily built security guy comes over patiently shaking his finger at him, then Dreadlocks swirls off, cartwheels, runs back to the stage and attacks the fence again. The security guard ambles over. Dreadlocks holds up his hands and goes charging off again, reeling back to duck under the tape at the side of the stage. He collapses to the floor and rolls around on the grass for a bit until the security guy reaches him and leads him back out to the front, but on the way he blunders into the tape, which snaps. The security guy sighs, and starts trying to tie the two bits of tape back together. Dreadlocks demands a beer from a girl at the front, and she reluctantly gives it to him, intimidated by his manic energy. He immediately pours it over his head. Then it's back to the stage for another attack on the security fence and another finger-wagging from the exasperated security guy. This happens many, many times. At one point Dreadlocks pulls off his trousers and throws them onto the stage. The security guy shakes his head in despair.

Just as a general principle, if you ever see a white guy with dreadlocks at a festival — stay away.

Still four hours to go before I play. No one around me knows any English so there's no one to chat with. I find myself getting increasingly nervous about what to expect from my gig, and spiralling into depression. When the rain starts up again I go and sit in Petr's van, where I watch people coming and going. Two young mini-skirted punk girls head towards the van and for a moment I wonder if they have recognised me and are coming to say hello, but then they veer off to the side and one of them throws up copiously behind a tree while the other one holds her hair out of the way. Another van pulls up and slithers across the wet grass, towing a trailer with a load of fencing on it. A disturbance catches my eye in the distance and I see the trouser-less dreadlocks guy being led out of the festival by one of the security crew, who then hurries back in to get on with his job. Dreadlocks waits a few seconds then staggers back, squeezes round the edge of the fence and goes back in. Five minutes later he is being led out again, but this time he is taken further away, almost up to van I'm in. I hope he doesn't see me.

As soon as the security guy is out of sight, Dreadlocks lurches back into the festival. The third time I see him, he is being led all the way down the hill and across the road, presumably on the theory that, like a mouse or a spider, if you take them far enough away they can't find their way back.

The rain stops and I wander up the steps to the 'VIP tent' up the hill. There are no VIPs there, if fact there's no one except for a couple of bored-looking girls behind the counter. I exchange one of my drinks tickets for a coffee in an attempt to revive and lift my mood. I can see the way this evening is heading and I have this internal dialogue going on: *You know what it's like in the Czech Republic but you came anyway, you idiot. You won't be able to talk to anyone all day, you will play for three people who won't understand a word of what you are singing, you will sell no CDs, you will be hungry and cold and wet, and eventually at the end of the night there will be a cramped dirty ex-communist hotel that will be more like an army barracks. You will get paid virtually nothing and you will leave tomorrow thinking, why am I doing this? Idiot. Idiot. Idiot.*

Just then I see Steve and Nelly from the Lurkers walking past the tent, obviously here a day early. English speakers! I fall on them like a starving wolf on a lamb.

Steve and Nelly are a couple of lads from Sunderland who I've known since my old mate Craig invited me up years ago for my first solo gigs in the North-East. It's great to see some friendly faces. We stand in the middle of the field with a beer, chatting and watching the general drunkenness around us. I tell Steve, 'I've a horrible feeling this is going to be another Spennymoor.'

We played together last winter in a god-forsaken freezing cold pub in this small town in the wilds of County Durham and no one came. Since then 'Spennymoor' has become the byword for a bad gig.

As we stand there chatting, three people approach. They're from the Basque country, where they've seen me play a couple of times and liked it so much that they've travelled five thousand kilometres – two days, sleeping under a tree last night – to come to this festival. They are really looking forward to seeing me play again.

Things are looking up: that's already three more fans than I had in Spennymoor.

Finally time is approaching for my gig. I leave Steve and Nelly and go to Petr's van to pick up my guitar and bag, and he trudges with me up the slope to the acoustic tent, where I pass my gear in over the tape to the security guy, who doesn't have much to do now Dreadlocks is no longer around. An old Czech singer/songwriter is onstage and there are plenty of people in the audience, all singing along and cheering wildly.

'Is old famous,' says Petr. 'Drinking songs.' He rolls his eyes.

Soon the old Czech guy is on his last song. There are only three strings left on his guitar and they're out of tune but it doesn't seem to bother him or the crowd. He leaves the stage, does an impressive sideways stagger as he ducks under the tape – methinks he knows whereof he sings – and the entire audience leaves the tent.

I'm left there with Petr and a couple of his friends. 'Typical Czech production,' says one of them, gesturing at the empty tent and the haphazard collection of equipment up on the makeshift wooden stage. 'Even the security is gypsy.'

Still ten minutes to go. Petr helps me carry a long wooden bench off the stage and I set it up just behind the tape barrier and spread my CDs and books along it in the forlorn hope that I will be able to sell some of them afterwards. Surprisingly, a scattering of people have started to gather in front of the stage and a couple ask me to have a photo with them. Maybe the gig won't be a Spennymoor after all.

A few strums on the guitar and a few words into the microphone does for a soundcheck and I'm surprised to find everything is sounding good. Even better, quite a few people are arriving now. SPS must have just finished, because after a few minutes the tent is packed. I'm getting enthusiastic applause at the end of every song. I feel my mood shoot up.

After a quick-fire fifty minute set and a four song encore I run from the stage, dripping with sweat and stand by the merch bench. The audience surges forward, through the security tape, and Petr swiftly sells all the CDs and books I've brought with me while I field requests for photos and autographs, and also try not to catch the eye of Dreadlocks, who has mysteriously reappeared and clearly liked the show. Steve and Nelly squeeze their way through the crowd. 'Bloody hell, Tim, that was something special!'

Slowly the crowd disperses. I hang around with Nelly and Steve for a while, then pack the guitar away and we go up to the VIP tent where Petr invites us over to his table where he is sitting with a bunch of friends and musicians. No one speaks much English, but after Petr has fetched a bottle of vodka from his van and passed it round, that doesn't seem to matter too much. I notice a disturbance and look over to see Dreadlocks being thrown out of the VIP tent by a security guy. On a positive note: he has somehow got his trousers back.

I must be enjoying myself: it's got much later then I expected. Before leaving Petr orders something to eat and asks me if I want anything. Even though there's a dish on the menu described as 'fried cheese in dough' which Steve – also a vegetarian – tells me is actually quite nice, I decide to hold out for the emergency sandwich when I get back to the hotel.

Twenty minutes through the dark country lanes and the van reaches Rokycany. Somewhere in this town is my hotel, but it takes a while to find it as we seem to have lost the bit of paper with the address. But eventually we're there, and Petr arranges to pick me up at twelve tomorrow and points out the restaurant next door where I can have breakfast at ten. Then he leaves me in the hands of a tired-looking receptionist who takes my passport details and hands me a set of three keys. 'Small key, room,' he says.

'Small key, small room?' I ask.

'Small key, big room!' he says.

And he's right. In fact it's two rooms, and a spacious bathroom. I hardly know where to settle down and eat the emergency sandwich. Funny: just when you think things are getting worse they start getting better.

14th August

I open the hotel front door and step outside to find my mate Rich – once guitarist for Amen and now guesting in Texas Terri's band – smoking a morning cigarette. He wanders over to the restaurant with me. It turns out the roads were much worse than expected last night and they had a very long and bumpy drive, getting in at five in the morning. He says, 'When we arrived I asked at Reception what time breakfast was and they told me, ten. I said, what – between eight and ten, or nine and eleven or something? – and they said: 'No. *Ten!*'

There's one big table laid out for us all, and within a few minutes everyone has arrived. I give Texas Terri the books and get introduced to the rest of the band, the German driver, and a friend of Rich's who came along for the ride. In front of us there are a couple of baskets of bread rolls and mini pots of jam, and a menu with some cooked options, all the ingredients carefully listed by weight, a hangover from the communist days. We all go for Number Four, which effortlessly lives up to its description of 'Omelette with cheese. 75g.'

Then Rich and I play Guess The Jam. The cherry is obvious because it has a picture of a cherry on it. The other one in the red carton confusingly turns out to be honey, so Rich puts that to one side and opens one with a picture of an indeterminate looking red fruit on it. 'Hmm, could be peach. Could be plum.' There is no clue in the name: *Merunka*.

'Let me try some of that,' I say and pick up a morsel on the edge of my knife. 'It's apricot!'

I remember when musicians having a jam meant something completely different.

I take a walk up the street with Tex and she tells me she is in a bad mood after the long drive last night because everyone else in the band was drinking and making a lot of noise while she was trying to sleep. I think she will enjoy my tour diary books. She says they have to get going for the festival in a couple of minutes, and why don't I hop in. It makes sense as it's on the way to the airport. Petr has already made a run to the airport this morning to pick up The Vibrators and should be at the festival again now so it will save him a journey.

I can't reach Petr on the phone but send him a text to let him know my plan, then go up to my room to pack up my gear. Not much left to pack, actually, after selling so many CDs last night. I jump in the back of the van with the band and we set off, soon seeing a sign saying 'Festival.' We drive up a hill and park just above the site, but something is bothering me. Petr made a few wrong turnings on the way back last night, but I'm sure we were driving for much longer than this. I look at the stage, exactly the same as the one they were preparing yesterday, and the line of merch stands and the tented area surrounded by metal fencing – all exactly the same as yesterday – and then I look up to the castle on the hill. There is no castle.

'Er, this is the wrong festival,' I say.

At first they don't believe me. In their position *I* wouldn't believe me. But the fact that we haven't left the outskirts of Rokycany and the festival is clearly in Zbiroh is the clincher, and we drive on.

'Jesus TV, I think you saved us some time there,' says Tex. 'It could have been hours before we realised.'

The band is travelling with a GPS system and so haven't bought a map, which is unfortunate as there is no signal here and we have to stop at a petrol station to ask for directions. The guy there attempts to send us back to the festival we have just come from, but eventually gets the message that we need to find Zbiroh. Following his arm signals we are soon heading through a twisty narrow road through a forest. It seems distinctly unpromising, and as it was dark when I was driven back last night I have no idea if we are going the right way.

'Have any of you seen that movie *Hostel?*' ask Rich.

I'm glad I'm not the only one who finds these forests creepy. 'You get the feeling all sorts of atrocities have been committed in there,' I say, gesturing at the towering wall of trees.

'*Atrocities*,' chuckles Rich, savouring the word.

We speed along, still unclear if it's the right direction, and I say, 'When I left home yesterday I had no idea I would end up on tour with Texas Terri Bomb, even if only for half an hour.'

Terri leans over from the seat in front.

'You better make up something really good about this for your *di-ary*. What are you gonna say, TV, what are you gonna say...?'

'Weeeell. I was on the road with Texas Terri and we left the hotel...and we drove to the wrong festival...'

'Yeah! Yeah! And then what happened?'

'Mmmm. Well, then we drove on and we got lost in the forest...'

'Great! Then what happened, TV? Then what happened?!!'

'Well, then...then...just a minute – that's Petr's van!'

And it is, beetling along in the other direction. 'Beep the horn!' I say to the driver. Truth be told, I'd been getting a bit worried about catching my flight and it's a big relief to see Petr.

The driver gives a tentative toot. 'No, REALLY BEEP it!' I shout. It suddenly occurs to me that our German driver may have momentarily forgotten we are in the Czech Republic and thinks Petr's van actually is the *Polizei*.

No matter, Petr has spotted us and pulled over to the side of the road. I leap into his van and explain the situation, then gesture to the others to follow us and we drive in tandem to Zbiroh, which turns out to be only a couple of kilometres away.

And that was my half hour on tour with Texas Terri Bomb.

We park next to the VIP area and Petr takes the band down to get their passes and drinks vouchers sorted out, even though he's not actually responsible for looking after them. He's got enough on his hands with the three bands he's booked: this morning he's already picked up The Vibrators from the airport and taken them to the hotel; next he has to drive me to the airport; then he comes back to drive The Vibrators from the hotel to the festival; then finally he has to go back to the airport to pick up Sham 69.

2 days, 3 bands, 400 kilometres.

While Terri goes down to the stage to put her CDs and T-shirts out on the merchandise stands, Rich and his mate are breaking into the first beer of the day in the VIP tent. Petr asks them if they want something to eat.

'Oh – no, thanks,' says Rich. 'I've already had 75 grams of breakfast. I don't think I'll be hungry *all day*.'

'Actually you only had 74 grams,' I point out. 'I had at least one gram of your jam.'

I remember when musicians talking about grams referred to something completely different.

'Have you ever tried a cheese and jam sandwich?' asks Rich. We're back on jam. 'It sounds disgusting but it's kind of nice.'

His friend says, 'Hey, have you ever done a peanut butter and sweet pickle sandwich?'

Done? It really does sound like they are talking about a drug cocktail.

Tex arrives back to gather her band together to go to the stage but it's time for me to go to the airport. We all say our goodbyes and Petr and I head towards the van. Just as we leave the tent, Petr turns back and says, 'I come back with Vibrators!'

I think Tex and I both do a double-take. What an exit line.

We hurtle down the motorway, a number of German tourists rapidly getting out of the way for us as they see the *Polizei* van bearing down on them in their rear-view mirrors. Along the way I peruse the cover of the CD Petr has given me of the young punk band he is managing. I point at the band's logo, the words *Spinaci Spendlik* inside a safety pin, and ask him what the name means. He says, 'It means *Safety Pin.*'

I'm at the airport with plenty of time to spare. Not many free places left on the plane, but I still manage to get a window seat right at the back. Everything's looking good.

The guy manning the X-ray machine at the gate looks up at me as the guitar goes through. 'You have some tools or something in there?' he asks. 'Pincers or something?'

Damn! The string clippers! For some reason they didn't get picked up by the X-ray on the way out, but now I can see they're going to be a problem.

'They're not even sharp, they couldn't possibly be dangerous,' I plead with the guy.

I demonstrate with my fingers how the clippers can only open a teeny bit. He says, 'Yes, I can see that on the machine. But you can't take them through.'

'Can I go back out and check the guitar in?' I ask.

'Yes, you can do that. If you have time before the flight.'

We both know there is not enough time before the flight.

He makes me open the guitar case and take the clippers out.

'You know, I really don't want to lose these,' I say. And I don't. They're my *favourite* string clippers.

The guy sighs. 'You can go and ask at the desk if they will let you take them through. I can't take the responsibility. You will have to leave the clippers here in the meantime though.'

'Okay,' I say. The guy takes the string clippers and puts them on top of the X-ray machine and I close up the guitar case and head for the desk. I know it is ridiculous but I am doing it anyway.

I explain the problem to the woman behind the desk. 'I see. Well, there's a slight delay on the flight. There is time to check your guitar in here, if you don't mind it going in the hold.'

'Okay. If that's the only way.'

'You agree to check in your guitar.'

'Yes.'

She calls a colleague and gets out a form I have to fill in, and fills in a form herself, then sets out some sticky labels with barcodes on to go on the forms and a label to attach to the guitar. Then she gets me to sign her form which has the string clippers down as a 'dangerous item,' then she gives me one of the labels and sends her colleague down to the X-ray machine to get the clippers. We all know it is ridiculous but we are doing it anyway.

The crew for the flight, who are still waiting to board, watch all this with interest, and when I get on the plane, one of the stewards asks me what band I'm in.

'I'm solo,' I say. 'I was playing a punk festival here.'

'What's your name?"

Usually I don't answer because I get sick of the reaction, *who?* – but this time I tell him and he says: 'TV Smith! Wow, I know you! *No Time To Be 21!* I'll have a word with you later.'

He asks what seat I'm in, so I show him my boarding pass, 26F. 'Actually, take a seat here,' he says, and gestures at the empty front row.

I've been bumped!

As I sit down at the window he leans in and says, 'Sorry we haven't got a spare meal, but we'll ply you with booze.'

'That's fine, I don't need a meal,' I say. I've had a 76g breakfast.

In fact, mid-flight, after the wine's been served he does rustle up a slice of tasty-looking quiche, but I have to turn it down because it's not vegetarian. Wouldn't want a UMM at 30,000 feet, not even in Business Class.

But I still get the mini bag of crisps, and a mini fruit scone AND the biscuit, and I don't even have to ask for it in a child's voice.

After a while the steward sits in the aisle seat and shows me his phone MP3 player with both Adverts albums on it. 'Legally downloaded and paid for!' he assures me.

He asks me how the festival went.

'Well, I thought it was going to be terrible, but it turned out to be great.'

'What's the name of it?'

'Bit embarrassing really: they called it "Old Punks Festival".'

'Nothing embarrassing about that. There are more of us old punks around than people think.'

He thanks me for chatting with him, then says he'll leave me to settle back.

So I settle back, and I get out my notebook, and I write this.

10. THE ONLY SONG IN THE WORLD (2011)

6th January

Only a couple of weeks ago I was stranded in Hamburg because all UK airports were closed due to the snow. The message was clear: flying and snow don't go together. It doesn't bother the Finns though. Here I am landing in Helsinki at eleven at night in a blizzard, snow streaking over the wings as we approach the airfield, the plane rocking in the fierce wind. As we bump across islands of packed ice on the way to the terminal, a phalanx of snowploughs head towards the runway to clear it for the next landing.

There are still problems though: we come to a stop and power down, then the boarding bridge steadfastly refuses to budge towards the plane so we can't get off. From my window seat I can see people in fluorescent jackets in there pulling levers and looking puzzled.

'Seems like the cold has affected the airbridge,' announces the captain as the shutters on it go down and the lights inside go out. 'Might as well take your seats for a few minutes.'

It's going to be more than a few minutes, I think, considering what would be involved to move the plane to another stand, or back far enough to let a coach in beside us. In a foot of snow. But then the lights flicker back on, the shutter goes up and the walkway moves gently forward and docks against the side of the plane. I overhear the captain remarking, 'The old switch-it-off then switch-it-on-again trick.'

The Stewardess announces, 'Please be especially careful when disembarking because obviously the airbridge has been exposed to the elements and could be slippery.' After the coldest winter for 100 years in England I have my snow legs, Finland can throw what it wants at me. All the same, the woman ahead of me takes a tumble two steps after getting off the plane and I remind myself not to get complacent.

After waiting at the outdoor bus station at the airport for ten minutes I look like I have been lightly frosted and it's a relief to see the city bus arrive. Thirty minutes later I'm standing in the city centre with my roller suitcase stuffed with 22 kilos of CDs and clothes, my shoulder bag and guitar. I'm struggling in the snow-laden gale with a soggy map, trying to figure out where my hotel is. Even more worryingly, it's an unmanned Omena hotel, which you can only get into by punching in a pre-assigned door code. It's a brilliant idea, but if something goes wrong there's no one to help. I've been on enough tours to know that if ever you're going to be unable to get into your hotel, it will be when it's minus six centigrade and bucketing down with snow.

But first, getting there. From the map it looks about a twenty minute walk but it takes considerably longer because the freshly-fallen snow is lying ankle deep, no one else around at this hour to tramp it down. Halfway up the hill I look around to see my roller-suitcase is dredging along a small mountain of snow. I have cleared a nice path along the pavement behind me.

But the door code works! 91884. I just have to remember it. So many numbers to remember on tour, I forget them all unless I write them down and it's annoying and painful in these sub-zero conditions to have to take my gloves off and ferret through all my documents. It would make things a lot easier if I could just keep the numbers in my head. Nine and one, opposite ends of the single digit numbers. Two eights, then a four – half of eight. That's got to be easy. When I pop out to see if I there's a shop open anywhere – there isn't – I've still remembered the code by the time I get back. I wrote it down just in case – I'm not a fool! – but even so, when I punch in the numbers from memory into the little black boxes next to the outer doors, the inner doors, the doors to my floor, and finally the doors to my room, and each time hear the whirr of the electronic lock opening it feels like a minor miracle.

7th January

Before leaving the hotel I get what I need for tonight's gig ready and realise I have forgotten to pack any stage vests to wear during the gigs. I have one short sleeved T-shirt to last ten days, everything else is warm weather gear which will be far too hot to wear while I play. There's a glimmer of hope: I'm in the studio for a few days next week between two batches of gigs so at least I have an address I can use. I send a text to Gaye asking her to urgently post a couple of vests there.

It's a lot easier getting back to the station than it was going the other way. It's downhill, for a start, and the snow's been trodden down by the morning commuters so I'm there in plenty of time before my train leaves. Armed with a coffee I look through my schedule and try and learn the numbers for my train today. Plenty of patterns in this lot: it's train number 133, leaving at 13:03 from platform 13. I have a reserved place in coach 3, seat 23. I'm pleased with myself for remembering all this by the time the train comes, and after I have stashed my suitcase in the corridor and put my guitar up on the rack and settled down I am quite surprised when a woman disturbs me claiming I have her seat. I show her my reservation.

'This is coach 2,' she says.

I arrive in Turku mid-afternoon, and as I get off the train I receive a phone call from promoter Matti, who tells me he's waiting under the big clock out the front. As we drive to the club he complains about the extreme weather and says his car has got stuck in the snow three times this week already. Turku is by the sea, so enjoys milder conditions than most of the country and usually the snow doesn't arrive until January or February, but this year it's been laying since early December.

I've played in Turku quite a few times, but Matti's club 'Graceland' is new to me. Matti hadn't heard of me until a friend suggested he came down to see me last year at another club in the town and he was so impressed he resolved to get me to play in his own place. He usually puts on more roots music rather than punk, he tells me, but is hoping for a decent turnout tonight as an interview I did recently with a local journalist has been printed and should help bring a few people.

We pull up outside the club, and it looks like a nice intimate place – a small low stage at one end and room for about a hundred people, a few tables and chairs scattered about, Elvis memorabilia up on the walls. Matti shows me to the room downstairs where I'll be sleeping. One side of the floor is awash with water dripping from the air conditioning pipes, but Matti tells me it's just from the heavy snow last night and is easing off now. He'll mop it up with some towels later. He also shows me the attached sauna and says I won't actually be able to come down here until mid-evening because he rents the rooms to a sauna club between six and eight.

Aware of the fact that we are directly underneath the bar I ask Matti if it's noisy down here – I'll need to get a fairly early night because I have to leave at nine tomorrow for my train. He admits that it's going to be loud until the club shuts at three, but shows me the telephone on the bar so I can call a taxi in the morning and save some time. He can't really drive me to the station himself because he lives on the other side of town and his car will probably be stuck in the snow. The phone looks vintage but is actually a modern copy, and he reassures me that it works just fine and shows me how to use it. And actually, the phone is ringing off the proverbial hook, and Matti is continually fielding enquiries for the gig tonight. 'Looks like we're going to have a sell out,' he says. Then he drives home for a couple of hours to clear the snow off his roof.

Which leaves me alone with a pot of coffee and a wi-fi connection so I can catch up on my emails. Soon after Matti returns some rockabilly guys also arrive and head downstairs – apparently these are the members of the sauna club. Another guy wanders in and sits by me. He reaches into a bag and presents me with a book of poetry he has written – translated into English, he hastens to tell me. He has read the article in the paper, where I mentioned that the first time I'd heard of Turku it was referred to as 'the arsehole of Finland,' and says that actually the city has the biggest underground scene in the whole of the country. 'Helsinki and Tampere are big media centres with television and radio stations,' he says, 'so people who want to get involved in that sort of thing move there. But here it's about real life.'

Just then a couple of the rockabilly guys, naked apart from white towels round their waists and leather boots on their feet, come up the stairs with cigarettes in their mouths, and go outside in the blizzard to smoke.

The audience starts to trickle in, and as I have nowhere else to go until the sauna is over I hang around by the bar and chat with them. One guy asks me what Gaye is doing now, and tells me he once saw a small ad in the Finnish music magazine Soundi saying, *Wanted: girlfriend who looks like Gaye Advert.*

Someone else invites me to sit at his table and offers to buy me a beer. I say I'll have a pint of my favourite Finnish beer, *Koff.* It's my favourite because of the way you say it. *Koff!* And you still get the beer. He comes back with it, and starts to tell me that it's very dangerous out on the streets at the moment. After the extreme cold, it's warmed up to just below freezing, and a lot of the giant icicles that have formed on the edges of the roofs are falling.

'What a way to go!' I laugh, 'Impaled by a giant icicle!'

He remains serious. 'Don't say I didn't warn you.'

Andy, the sound guy comes over. 'What time do you want to start?' he asks.

I'd like to start now, and the people I'm sitting with are keen for me to start too, but Matti thinks I should hold off for another hour.

'I'll be ready,' says Andy.

'I'll be drunk,' I joke, gesturing at my swiftly disappearing beer.

'So will I,' says Andy

He's serious.

The sauna guys have gone so I nip downstairs and get a bit of quiet to prepare for the gig. When I come back up again, the people at the table I was sitting at earlier start a round of applause that goes round the entire room. I'd better start the concert then.

What a great way to begin a tour: a two hour set in front of a sold out club with everyone listening, then lots of CD and book sales afterwards at the little table I've set up next to the stage. After chatting with most of the audience for more than an hour I go downstairs to change into a dry T-shirt, and while I'm there I quickly check my emails and see one from the journalist who wrote the article about tonight's gig.

'Hope you had an excellent gig in Graceland, Turku, the arsehole of Finland,' he writes. 'I tried to be there but got turned away at the door, because it was sold out...'

Ah.

Most of the people still upstairs could now be best described as 'casualties' and it's not long before three o'clock arrives, the last stragglers are shown the door and I go down to my basement room, where the air conditioning is still dripping away, the fresh towel placed underneath the leak already soaked. Looks like I'll only have about five hours sleep, so I don't bother unfolding the couch to make a bed and just stretch out on it as it is, pull the duvet cover over myself and drift off to sleep to the sound of Chinese water torture…*splat…spat…splat…*

8th January

Getting out of bed and stepping in a puddle of freezing water is not the ideal start to a day. The snow melt has crept towards the couch and I have to negotiate through patches of dry floor to pack my things.

Upstairs, the period-piece phone is also a not-working phone. I feel like someone in an old movie as I jab repeatedly at the cradle but there's still no dial tone. The number for the taxi firm Matti has given me has no country or area prefix so won't work on my mobile. There's only one thing for it…

It's a good job I gave myself an extra half hour for the worst case scenario, for that is exactly what I'm in. 2.2 Kilometres to the station according to Google map, that's 29 minutes by foot in normal walking conditions, and I have 30 minutes before my train leaves and streets full of snow to contend with. I can see my chances of getting to Kokolla slipping away. Literally slipping, as I negotiate my roller bag over the packed ice, grateful for every gritted section where I can increase my speed. The nearer I get to the station the less the pavements have been gritted and the more treacherous they become so that on the final stretch I can see the big clock above the building at a couple of minutes before ten – seven minutes to go before my train leaves – but the pavements are so slippery that I feel like I'm moonwalking: my feet are pounding down but the drag from my bag is pulling me inexorably backwards like I'm in a bad dream. I've broken out into a sweat but I have no time to take off my scarf or gloves. When I arrive at the platform at the exact moment my train pulls in, I am the hottest man in Finland. Suddenly rolling in the snow seems like a good idea.

Coach 2, seat 35. Easy! Two plus three equals five.

Two hours later the train passes Toijala, where right now my friend Japi is in his studio working on mixes for my new album. I text him a hello. Then I change trains in Tampere and it's another three hours to Kokkola where I'll be playing tonight.

A long bag-drag through Kokolla's main street brings me to my hotel, just around the corner from the club, where I'm given the key to room 404. Four-zero-four, the well-known internet error message, child's play! This remembering numbers idea is easy when you home in on it, there are patterns all over the place. The USB dongle the receptionist gives me to use the internet crashes my computer so I take it back down to the desk and reluctantly pay up the eight euros for a wi-fi pass. I don't regret it – the room is bloody cold and it's worth the money just to find out on Google translations that the switch in the bathroom marked *Lattialämmitys* means 'underfloor heating.'

Over at the venue, soundcheck is delayed because a darts tournament has only just finished. When the contestants hear I'm English, they all come over and show me their scores. Promoter and sound engineer Juhi suggests I come back in an hour, which will give the darts club time to clear away the boards and for him to figure out how to work the new mixing desk he's just had installed.

On my return soundcheck goes swiftly and as I'm not supposed to play until after eleven I go back to the hotel yet again to kill a few hours on the computer. I've been in the room for a while when I realise that even with the underfloor heating on in the bathroom it really is cold. I'm shivering! There's no thermostat and the radiator is barely functioning so I go down to Reception and ask, suddenly feeling very English, if it's possible to, er, switch the heating up a bit? 'No,' says the receptionist, 'I can't do that. But I can give you a different room.'

And the radiator works in this one. Excellent! Except that I went to all that trouble to learn 404. I will almost certainly try and get into the wrong room when I return at the end of the evening.

Back at the venue there are already a few people in. I recognise one guy at the bar, though I can't remember where from and go over and have a chat with him. He reminds me he's seen me here a couple of years ago. And in Helsinki. And Tampere. He even came to see me in London last year. It's ringing a bell now: I remember chatting to him before the London gig, which was at the Bull & Gate. It was pretty poorly attended, and when I didn't see him again afterwards I worried that he was disappointed that the gig was less exciting than the ones I play in Finland. 'That was the one where not many people came, wasn't it?' I ask.

'I don't remember anything,' he says. 'I was too drunk.'

A couple of other guys join in the conversation, which inevitably gets round to the melancholy nature of the Finns. One of them tells me that a friend of his moved to Los Angeles and started suffering from depression. He went to a doctor who discussed various drug treatments. Meanwhile the nurse was looking through his medical records and interrupted: 'Don't bother with medication. He's not depressed, he's Finnish.'

In front of the stage people are dancing to the records the DJ is playing, always a worrying thing before I play live. I hate to spoil their fun. But when I start, soon after 11:30, there's a politely favourable response to the first song and it continues like that throughout the set, never really building to any kind of climax. I remember from last time I played this venue that we really are out in the sticks here and people are very reserved, so any positive reaction is encouraging. Afterwards everyone crowds round at the merch table and one by one they tell me how much they enjoyed it.

At three in the morning, aware that I'm going to the studio tomorrow, I decline offers to go on to 'the next place' for more to drink and make my way around the corner to my hotel. My hotel seems to be 'the next place' – the bar in the basement is full and a lot of people from the gig are outside smoking and chatting in the lobby. I manage to sneak my way to the lift without getting spotted.

9th January

Snow ploughs are out on the streets, but they haven't cleared the pavements and soon after leaving the hotel I am dragging along several tons of snow with my bag. The train gets me into Tampere by four in the afternoon and I check into the Omena hotel there, where I'll be staying the next four nights while I work on the album. The door code is 62751 – not bad. There's the six, then the two to signify the gap between the following two numbers on either side of the six, then one for 'done.' It's a nice pattern on the keypad too.

I pop around the corner to a supermarket and buy some tofu, salad and fruit as well as some chilled soya snacks to stock up the fridge in the room and give myself a break from what has been an almost exclusively bread and cheese diet since I got to Finland. Then it's off to the station for the journey out to Japi's studio in Toijala, half an hour down the line towards Helsinki.

A woman's voice over the tannoy announces: *The inter-city train to Helsinki arrives, and leaves, from platform two.* I hadn't considered the possibility that it might leave from a different platform than it arrived at but now she's mentioned it, it's good to know.

Japi picks me up from the station and we drive over to the studio, which his dad built in the basement of the family home when he used to record programmes for a local radio station. It's an old wooden house in the forest on the edge of town, other houses scattered about under the snow-laden trees. As we drive up, Japi's dad is shovelling snow out of the way so we can get down to the basement. There's a slight thaw on and the surface is treacherously slippery. As we step carefully down the slope to the door I look up to check I'm not about to be impaled by a giant icicle. I was warned.

Then it's on with some mixing, and I get the late train back for tofu, beer and sleep.

10th January

Studio.

11th January

Studio.

12th January

Things went so well that there's no real need for me to go back to Toijala before my gig today – which is good, because soon after I wake up I get a text from Japi saying he's gone down with the flu and is 'feeling like a lobster. A lobster in boiling water.'

My initial plan is to visit the Moomin Museum instead, something I've been meaning to do ever since my first visit to Tampere years ago, but somehow I get swamped in emails and before I know it, it's time to leave for soundcheck at the Telakka club. I pack all the things I'll need for tonight into my shoulder bag so I don't have to come back before the show. Luckily the vests arrived at the studio yesterday, just in time. Gaye had wrapped them in a plastic bag from a vet, and on it is printed: *This bag can be used as a poop scoop.* Well, touring can get boring. Maybe I will feel like going out and doing a bit of poop-scooping later.

Soundcheck is over in ten minutes, then slowly my old friends trickle in – Jukka and family, tour agent Harri, and Tiina from Punk Lurex and all her friends. Jukka asks me how the album mixing is going and whether I'll play any new songs tonight. I say I'll try but it's always hard to squeeze them in when I only have an hour like here. 'It's true,' says Jukka, 'you always get requests for 'One Chord Wonders' or 'Gary Gilmore's Eyes' but you never get people standing at the front shouting, *PLAY NEW STUFF!*'

Actually I stretch the set to ninety minutes and play five new songs, which seem to be the best received of all of them. After one of them I mention that I have been in the studio working on my new album. 'And where? London? Los Angeles? No… Toijala!' and that gets a big laugh and a cheer, and chants of *Toijala! Toijala!* break out during the rest of the evening. Toijala is not renowned for being the most exciting town in Finland.

After the gig I sit having a beer with some of the audience for a while, the the 'last orders' lights flash and a plan is formulated to go over to Klubbi, just the other side of the car park. Just then the manager of the Telakka comes up and tells me in halting English that the hotel has phoned to say I need to check in before two because Reception will be closed after that and I won't get in. This is a bit confusing. The Omena has no Reception and I will get in – 62751, the magic number. Tiina translates for me and it becomes apparent that the manager didn't know Harri had put me in the Omena so he booked me a hotel too. This results in much amusement and ribbing from the people around our table who start calling me TV 'Two Hotels' Smith.

Honestly, you wait ages for a hotel and then two come along at once.

'So…' says one of our party to me, 'Two rooms. How are you going to disintegrate?'

I don't know. I just don't know how I'm going to disintegrate.

13th January

Somewhere on the way to Lahti I suddenly remember my last time there: a great, very late, gig but afterwards a depressing little hostel to sleep in. I look through the schedule from Harri to see where I'm staying. Could it be the same place? Originally the accommodation details said 'tba somewhere nearby' but I asked to know in advance because my train arrives at three in the afternoon and soundcheck isn't until eight. I don't want to be stranded on the street for five hours in sub-zero temperatures and Lahti isn't exactly awash with coffee bars and restaurants to while away the time. In fact, I failed to find any kind of city centre at all last time I was here. When Harri found out the hotel name – *Matkakoti Patria* – I added it on to the schedule, and now I try and remember if that was where I stayed last time. From the map it looks like it probably is.

It is. And I've been in the snow ringing the bell for some time before I see the sign 'Back at four.'

Can I have my spare hotel from yesterday now please?

The only place I can find open to wait in is the bar above the venue where I'm playing tonight, which at this hour seems to be populated mainly by local drunks and my request for a coffee gets a raised eyebrow. I raise an eyebrow too when I taste it, but it only costs one euro.

Back at the hostel at four, I remember the little old lady behind the reception desk, who runs the place with her son Gordon, who is often mentioned but rarely seen. 'What have you got there?' she says, looking at the guitar, then asks my name and chatters about how many 'troubadors' used to stay in this hostel when a bar called Molly Malone's was still going. She crosses the 'TV' from TV Smith off the list of guests and replaces it with 'Tim.'

'Now then, where has Gordon put you, Tim?' she murmurs, perusing her ledger, as if Gordon and me are the best of mates.

He's put me in Room 11, which would be easy enough to remember but I don't need to because I have a key with it written on. 'Here's your little room,' says the lady, holding the door open for me. And little it is, as well as being free from the encumbrance of toilet or shower – although the toilet is right across the narrow corridor from me: an advantage in that it's nearby, a disadvantage in that the door slams so I will presumably be woken up by it on a regular basis in the night.

While the melting snow pools across the floor from my suitcase I look despondently around. Somehow I feel far from civilisation. I read the notice on the back of the door: Check out time is at ten. Hmmm…

I march back up to the reception desk.

'Yes, Tim?'

'I have two questions: one, do you have wi-fi in the rooms?' Even as I say it, I know it's ridiculous to even ask.

'Well, er – do you have a, er, a...' She says a long Finnish word which she immediately realises I won't understand. ''Well, never mind. We used to have a, er, a *steady* in this room here, but now he's gone.'

I see.

'The other question is: can I get a late check-out? I probably won't be in until three or four in the morning.'

This seems to cause an inordinate amount of worry, and she looks through the ledger with some concern. 'Let's see now. Oh, dear, Gordon's got someone already booked in your room at 12:30.'

Bloody Gordon.

She taps her pencil, and finally gives out a sigh. 'I suppose I *could* move them to another room. I'll have to tell Gordon though!'

She draws a little arrow from room eleven to room thirteen and then fixes me with a piercing look. 'If you're coming in at three in the morning you'd better be very quiet.'

Yes Mum.

The venue is only just around the corner, and the contract allows one hour for load in – hardly necessary in my case, as 'load in' means 'walk in' – so I leave it to the last minute to go over there. The soundman already has a microphone for the vocals set up, and another one at guitar height. I tell him I don't need the second one because I plug the guitar straight in to the P.A. but he tells me it's set up for 'the other guy' who has already done his soundcheck. I didn't know there was going to be another guy. Soundcheck takes twenty seconds, then as there is no mention of the promised meal in a nearby restaurant I go back to the hotel, buying a sandwich from the local supermarket on the way. Nothing is more depressing than clubs before they open, not even cheap hotels. As I pass Reception the lady darts out from behind her desk. 'I've told Gordon about you sleeping late,' she says, 'so now it's up to him if he wakes you up or not.'

You'd better not try it, Gordon.

The lady is actually very sweet and friendly, and also well educated – I've heard her speaking fluent Russian as well as English and Finnish on the phone – and the hostel is clean, certainly. It's just I'd rather be in a room where the bed doesn't shake when someone down the hall shuts their door.

Back at the venue, there are a few people in already and I hear someone shout my name as I walk through. It's Robert, who is often at my gigs in Finland, and who's always fun to hang around with. 'I'm playing support!' he says.

He's never played a solo gig before, but after a long drunken night recently he suddenly decided he was going to try it. He phoned up the venue here and the manager said yes. He plans a twenty minute set of acoustic GG Allin covers. GG Allin was notorious for his extreme and provocative sets which often involved removing all his clothes and relieving himself in front of, or on, the audience. 'Just don't shit on the stage,' I say.

He doesn't, but he feels like shit, coming back to the dressing room after his set bemoaning how terrible it was. 'Stupid idea! Never again!'

Robert's discomfort is a bit of a relief to me, because it takes the pressure of my own nerves. I'm feeling strangely anxious about tonight's show, and have spent the last couple of hours feeling like I'm on the edge of a panic attack, much more severe than usual. Or maybe it was just the bad coffee earlier? As usual though, the nerves evaporate as soon as I hit the stage. The first half hour of the show is close to perfection, everyone paying attention, listening carefully, exploding into applause when the song finishes. I get the feeling that the songs during this opening section are among the best versions I've ever played. The next hour is pretty good too. The mood is broken at one point when someone comes up to the stage with an acoustic guitar and asks me to sign it. You might think he'd have waited until the end – it's not like I'm going anywhere.

Then I chat with the people and drink a few beers. The guy with the guitar comes back and asks me to write the first verse of 'Gary Gilmore's Eyes' on the back of it, which I proceed to do, except my concentration right now isn't all it could be and I lose my way with the lyrics. The guy looks a bit disappointed to see that the first verse of my hit single on his guitar now finishes: *oops, that's wrong but to be honest I've been on stage for two hours and I really can't do this right now.*

Eventually the crowd thins and I make my way back to the hostel, where I creep in ever so silently. Except for that slamming-the-guitar-against-the-door thing while I was looking for my key.

14th January

Gordon – it must be him – is hoovering, mainly in the corridor outside my door and the rooms either side. Not that it makes much difference, I've been awake on and off since soon after eight when the first guests started noisily getting up and leaving. At tonight's gig in Pori I'm not even supposed to get on stage until midnight. Maybe I'll just forget about the idea of sleep altogether.

Three trains will get me to Pori by late afternoon and while I'm waiting for one change, back at Tampere again, and watching one of the endless snow ploughs diligently shifting the newly fallen snow from the platform, the thought occurs to me: what do snowplough drivers do the rest of the year?

A stopping train to Pori and it's already dusk as we pull into the station. I'm waiting with my bags at the end of the carriage, looking at my directions for the hotel as the train comes to a stop, and a guy behind me says something to me in Finnish. 'I'm sorry,' I say, 'I don't understand. I'm English.'

'I said, have you maybe left something behind on the rack there, a guitar or something?'

I look back into the carriage with a sudden surge of panic about what so nearly could have been. I know it's going to happen someday and today it nearly did. The Finnish guy may still be wondering why he got hugged by a stranger.

I remember Pori. I slipped over in the snow here a year ago. As I negotiate the ungritted pavements leading from the station I can easily imagine my humiliation being repeated. This is the slipperiest city in Finland.

To my relief I've been put in a good hotel today, so I have the chance to shower and catch up on emails, in a comfortable room without Gordon nosing around outside, before heading round the corner for soundcheck at the Monttu bar, a club I've never played before. It's going to be a late one: the schedule has me onstage at midnight for an hour, then a local support band playing after me. I'm glad it's that way around as I have to leave at nine tomorrow for my train to Helsinki and although I've established that sleep is an optional luxury on tour, a few hours would be nice all the same. The schedule also shows an hour to load in at 16:00, an hour for the support band to soundcheck at 17:00 and an hour for me to soundcheck at 18:00, but when I turn up at 18:45 there's no one in the club, just a few instruments scattered over the stage. One of the other band wanders in and tells me that the sound man won't be here until nine and the club doesn't open until eleven. Back to the hotel then.

When I get back to the club at nine-thirty the sound guy is at his desk. He tells me the other band have done their soundcheck and he's ready for me. I play a bit and everything sounds fine but he can see I'm not happy.

'No, it sounds great,' I reassure him, 'it's just…this microphone. It stinks!'

It is so foul that I am on the point of gagging every time I take a breath to sing another line. With a smile he changes the microphone, muttering, 'Too many rock'n'roll musicians,' then we soundcheck again and everything smells fine.

The sound guy looks at his watch. 'So you want to play first?'

'Well, yeah, midnight – that's already late enough isn't it?'

'Gigs are very late here,' he says. 'I mean, I think you are the main guy, not this other band, so normally you should play last. It's fine by me if you want to go on first, but I don't know what the promoter will think.'

I look at my schedule. 'It says here that the support plays after me, so he must know. I guess the promoter reads the contract.'

The support band are in the cramped dressing room and also surprised about their headlining status, which they've only just found out about. They try and persuade me to go on second, and explain they are just a loud, thrash punk band who are going to 'fuck the audience up,' Now I'm even more glad I'm going on first. They are bemoaning the fact their singer didn't bother to turn up to the soundcheck. Instead he texted: *Just get on with it, assholes.*

'He's crazy,' the drummer tells me. 'He plays in punk bands, but his job is – ah, what do you call it? Where you, zzzzzit, slit dead bodies open?'

The drummer talks quite a lot. He makes me write my name up on the wall next to theirs – I think this is the first time I have written on a dressing room wall in thirty-five years – and tells me he is into old school punk rock and they are going to play a lot of punk rock tonight. Well, all they've learned, about twenty minutes. It's their second gig – their first really, because at the other one their singer was ill and couldn't come. They played anyway. They have one song called 'Anarchy Finland,' and the lyrics are 'Anarchy! Finland!' repeated a lot of times. They want to know all about UK punk rock and whether I have met John Lydon and Lemmy and Joey Ramone and Sid Vicious, and they are drinking far too much far too quickly.

The singer arrives and seems like a nice guy. I have a feeling the drummer might have been, ah, *projecting* somewhat when he talked about how crazy he is. 'Yes, I am autopsy assistant,' he explains soberly, and introduces his girlfriend. 'And so is she.'

It's nice to have a common interest.

The promoter arrives and I like him immediately. He also tells me he's a friend of Jukka and is in a band on his label called The Wolfmen. Out of earshot of the band he tells me, I put you on first because I didn't want you to have to play after these idiots have destroyed the place.

There is some negotiating about when I play and for how long. He thinks I should wait a bit and play for an hour, but it's midnight already and I'm tired of waiting so I suggest I go on earlier and play longer.

Even though the guys in the other band are fun, I'm not really here for the kind of punk rock they're aiming for, and I've been finding the endless noisy chatter in the dressing room distracting so it's good to get out of there and on stage where the people who actually know what I am about are waiting for me. A very nice gig, a responsive crowd, and I play for ninety minutes – a bit shorter than usual but the thought of the band playing next and an early start tomorrow focuses my mind on not going on too late.

Then I move my stuff out of the way so the band can start. The promoter comes back to the dressing room to thank me and I pack my guitar away, steeling myself for the punk rock attack that is about to occur onstage.

It's already been an hour since I finished my set and I really should sneak away and get some sleep but it would be rude not to watch at least some of the band. Shouldn't they be on by now? And how come the singer is in the dressing room still, and so is the soundman, and the promoter is getting his coat on and getting ready to leave?

'Have they already played?' I ask the soundman.

'The drummer can't play, he is too drunk. I mean he absolutely can *not* play.'

I turn to the singer. 'So you're not playing at all?'

'Nope,' he smiles.

He seems to be taking it very well. I suppose handling dead bodies all day gives you a certain perspective on things.

So, it looks like I could achieve four or five hours sleep after all. The singer walks me back to my hotel, says he hopes we meet again and shakes hands. I know where that hand has been.

15th January

Watching the weather on the television in the breakfast room I see that overnight lows for tonight are forecast as minus thirty in some parts of Finland. Makes the coldest

British winter for one hundred years look a bit lightweight.

It's a good job I've booked a taxi because as the driver takes my suitcase the handle comes off, which would have made it tricky to roll the kilometre to the station. In fact, inspecting the bent and broken rivet holes at the base of the handle it's clear that this is a roller bag that will roll no more. Sad to see it go really: while other suitcases I've taken on tour with me have barely lasted a few months, this one has survived more than five years of heavy gigging – until now. I guess the combined job of being a suitcase and a snowplough was finally too much for it. The only good thing I can think about this situation is that at least it happened on the last day of the tour so I only have to carry it around for twenty four hours before I go home and buy a new one. If it had happened on the first day it could have been a problem.

I open my suitcase and put the handle inside. I know it's ridiculous, but that handle's coming home with me.

I struggle onto the icy platform towards the train. On the horizon, where the rails join, the sun rises in a drift of golden mist. The sky is an expanse of pale shimmering powder blue and the land as far as the eye can see is sparkling white, the trees like frozen fireworks.

I change trains in Tampere, and the connection to Helsinki is very crowded, with nowhere to put my guitar or crippled suitcase, the racks above me already full. I think it's insider knowledge in Finland that you put your suitcase on the rack above someone else's seat. That's why ten minutes into the journey I'm being dripped on by the snow melt from a suitcase that isn't mine. Meanwhile the fat man in the seat next to me snores on.

Today the plan is to go to the studio in the afternoon with a Finnish ska band called The Valkyrians and record a ska version of *Gary Gilmore's Eyes*, an idea they hatched up when we met coincidentally at my German booking agency's office in Berlin a couple of months ago. In the evening I'll play my gig in a club called Bar Loose, a venue I've never been in before but which seems to have a good reputation. So, let's have a look at my schedule and find out where the hotel is. It's an Omena again, not that far away from the one I stayed in at the beginning of the tour, but far enough to mean – my bag has no handle – that I will need to get a taxi. Tonight's lucky number that will get me in to the hotel: 92982. Quite a nice one to learn, good rhythm. And room number 206 – so close to last night's 236, and even closer to Tampere's 201. So close that it's all becoming a bit of a blur. I'd better write them down.

I get out of the taxi and head for the keypad, pleased with myself that I've remembered the number, but disappointed when it doesn't let me in. A second attempt also fails so I look it up in my notebook. It's correct. I try it again with the notebook propped open just in case I've wrongly remembered the number I thought I'd remembered rightly. But no.

This does present a problem. Particularly as it's minus twelve degrees. Could it be… could it possibly be…that my schedule from the agency has the address of the wrong Omena and it should actually be the other one in Helsinki where I stayed in last time? Normally it wouldn't take long to get there and find out, but I have a shoulder bag, a guitar, and a suitcase with no handle, and the pavements are sheet ice. However, when there is no alternative…

But the number doesn't work in the other hotel either.

Ummm. Plan C. Ummm. I'll have to phone Harri, even though he probably won't be at the agency because it's Saturday. Although…oh dear, I just remembered that when I saw him in Tampere he told me that on Friday he was leaving for a few days holiday in France.

Ah. Plan D. Plan D…

The venue isn't far either. I'll struggle over there and use their phone.

I struggle over there. They're shut.

Come in Plan E. I'll be meeting the Valkyrians outside the Omena at three – that's only about half an hour. I can wait it out until then. I slither my way back, with frequent stops to swap the guitar and suitcase between numb hands, and try the code again. Of course it doesn't work, but while I'm trying I notice the sign for an emergency phone number above the keypad. Not much credit left on my phone, but no choice. The first time I ring I get a recorded voice saying something in Finnish, then in English: *This number has not been allocated. Please check the number and try again.*

Could I have put in the wrong phone number? I try again, taking extra care to make sure every digit is right and get the same message. What a useful emergency line! And it managed to swallow up my last couple of quid credit so now I can't phone anyone.

Only twenty minutes until the band arrive, so I sit it out in the pizza place next door with a one euro coffee. At one point I go to use the loo and find myself in a corridor linking through to the hotel. Good Lord, there's the door I've been trying to open for the last hour and here I am on the inside of it. True, I can't get through the next door that leads to the stairs up to the rooms, but there is a phone with *Omena* written on it. I pick it up. It rings at the other end. A woman's voice comes on the line and says, 'Omena.'

And when I say hello it turns out she understands English, and she asks for my room number and name and then makes a sound that indicates she has sorted out the problem!

'Booked in for one night, tonight?'

'That's right,' I say, relieved.

'In Omena hotels you can't get into the rooms until four,' she says. 'The code will work after that.'

The coffee is cold but the Valkyrians have arrived and we don't have to take the train to the studio as expected, they have a car! Not much room in it by the time the four of us and my suitcase and guitar have squeezed in, but we're going by car, and by the time they bring me back the hotel will be open.

I didn't know what to expect from a ska version of Gary Gilmore's Eyes, but when the band play back the demo they've recorded I am surprised to find that not only is it a completely different arrangement but that it also has different chord changes and is in a different key. It causes me some confusion when I go into the vocal booth to sing it, in fact I get so lost I have to break off and fetch the lyrics. After the incident signing the guitar the other night, this is the second time I have forgotten the lyrics to my most famous song in the last few days. Honestly, you wait ages to forget the lyrics to…

I get it after three takes and am pleased to hear that the finished thing sounds very good, a strange and unexpected collision of styles. Only the Finns could come up with such a ridiculous idea and make it work.

A couple of the band drive me back to the Omena while the others carry on working on the song. One of the guys gets out and helps me with my bags over to the door.

'It's got to work now,' I tell him, 'but maybe you could hang around just in case there's a problem and I need to borrow your phone.' He nods. 'I even learned the number, 72872,' I say.

Or is it?

'No hang on, I'd better check.'

It's 92982. I murmur the numbers a few times to myself to try and re-establish the pattern in my head, then put the notebook away. But when I reach for the keypad I've already forgotten it. I am really quite tired. I get the book out again and recite the code to my new friend, who is looking at me with pity, and he punches the numbers in as I read them out. The door clicks open, we go in, and then he puts the code into the keypad by the internal door (without me having to tell it to him again – bastard) and finally we say goodbye. By the time I reach the top of the stairs I have still remembered the number and I successfully get into the second floor corridor, but when I get to Room 201 and put the code into the keypad outside the door it doesn't work.

I check my notepad again. I'm in Room 206.

Then there's just time for a quick change of strings before soundcheck. It takes longer than usual because on the first string my string-winder breaks. It is national Things Going Wrong Day.

The club looks good, the sound guy tells me he has seen me before in the Semifinal and is looking forward to it. Soundcheck goes fast and sounds excellent and I feel myself starting to get excited. The sound guy comes over and tells me that later there will be some beer and vegetables and stuff in the backstage for me.

Vegetables? Stuff?

Still a couple of hours to go before the place opens so I go back to the Omena. When I leave again for the club it's minus twenty outside and my eyes freeze over.

Oh yes, there's that feel in the club – it's going to be a good one. Robert is there with a couple of friends. He appears to have recovered from the GG Allin experience and is enjoying the band on stage before me. 'I see tonight you have a decent support band, unlike in Lahti,' he says, a note of bitterness in his voice.

My friend Tommi, who first suggested I come to Finland years ago, has arrived with various friends and band members. Pointing out the 80's glam influence of the support band, he tells me that his band will be introducing a song by Mud into their next gig. '*Dynamite*. We will be singing it in Finnish.'

'Really? How do you say *dynamite* in Finnish? Or do you sing that word in English?'

'No, we sing it in Finnish. "*Deh-nah-meh-teh.*" It sounds terrible. That's why we do it.'

The Valkyrians have arrived back from the studio and are over by the bar, talking excitedly about putting Gary Gilmore's Eyes on the new EP and pushing it to radio stations. 'If there's anything you ever need in Finland, we will help,' says singer Angster. 'I give you my phone number. If you ever have a problem with your hotel, or a gig gets cancelled, or anything at all, we have friends all over Finland who will come and help. You just call.'

The support band are finishing up, and telling the audience to enjoy my set. 'We like TV Smith! He's a great guy!'

And then I'm on stage and for the next ninety minutes I'm lost in what I do best.

When the set is over I stay on stage a while, chatting to people and selling my last few CDs. I'm particularly glad about not having to take them home with me, considering my suitcase has no handle. The manager of the club comes up and says how much he enjoyed my set, and leans in to tell me that he's put the stuff backstage for me.

The stuff?

Backstage there is a chair in the middle of the room with a plate piled up with:

2 oranges.
3 large pears.
3 large green apples.
1 bunch of grapes (green)
1 bunch of grapes (red)
3 bananas
1 pineapple.

There's a piece of paper propped up on the fruit bonanza, and written on it in red felt pen: TV SMITH.

When I see the manager later, I say, 'I have to ask – why the fruit?'

'Oh there was something about fruit and vegetables on your rider, so we thought we would give you a selection. Just eat what you can!'

Maybe a slight misunderstanding of the concept of being a vegetarian. I take a banana for breakfast, leave the rest and write *Kiitos* ('thank you') on the paper.

And sadly, my tour of Finland is just about over. I put on my scarf, gloves, hat and jacket and haul my guitar and shoulder bag out onto the icy streets towards the Omena. It will be strange going back to normal walking when I get back to London tomorrow, I'm so used to the Finland plod. The pavements here require a whole different attitude. There's the top layer: a soft brown, powdery drift of finely ground-up grit and ice. Then there's the white hard bumpy frozen snow underneath that. The bottom layer is two inches of hard frozen clear ice, sometimes unexpectedly rising into an irregular ridge where there has been a run-off from a gutter, or dipping where it's been chipped away or briefly melted; sometimes clearing altogether to reveal a bare patch of slippery pavement. Apart from these patches, nowhere you walk is flat, and every step is a mystery as to what surface your foot will land on. You curl your toes inside your shoes and clump down, aware that at any moment your foot could go skittering out from under you.

As I trudge along I have this song going round and round in my head. The lyrics go: *nine-two-nine-eight-two, nine-two-nine-eight-two, di-di di di-di, nine-two-nine-eight-two.*

It's not much of a song. It won't be a hit and it's not going to change people's views about anything, but as the lock on the outer door, the inner door, the second floor, and finally my room whirr open, to me it's the only song in the world.

11. GET HIM (2011)

<u>10th June</u>

As we land at Helsinki the temperature outside is 33 degrees centigrade, that's almost sixty degrees higher than when I was last here five months ago. I take the bus into the centre and then a taxi to the venue. The sun-drenched streets are decked with flags for Helsinki day this weekend. There's a Finnish language version of Summer In The City playing on the car radio.

The venue is a new one for me called Nosturin. It's a nice little club down on the waterfront, a part of town I've never visited before. Large windows running along one side of the room look across the harbour and out to sea. The support band are still getting their equipment on stage and no one seems in too much of a hurry even though the soundcheck should have started half an hour ago. It's too hot to rush around. There is some food ready in the kitchen, and now seems a good time to take advantage of it. The barman takes me in there and explains what is in the various bowls, apologising for his limited English. 'It's all vegetarian, except this one is fish. And this one is...er...'

'That looks like pasta?'

'Yes. With – er – that thing that makes you strong. That Popeye eats.'

Language barrier wot language barrier?

After soundcheck it's a ten minute walk up the road to the hotel, the same Omena where I stayed last time. I'm only momentarily confused when I get to the third floor to look for the room I've been assigned – 324 – and find the numbers only go up to 323. After a quick search through the fourth and second floors I notice another hotel block on the other side of the courtyard. That's where my room is.

Back at the venue there are a few people sitting out at tables on the small terrace, absolutely no one inside. I think tonight's gig may fall victim to the weather. It's just too hot to be inside a sticky club, and as the sun never sets here at this time of year the heat never really drops. Still, there are a few old friends and some faces I recognise from my past gigs in Finland. I have a chat with Tommi, Berja and Janne, part of my regular Helsinki crew, whose band Neverzillos will also be playing on the same bill as me tomorrow at a little independent festival called *Ketollaika*, which takes place on a farm way out in the countryside. The festival is actually the reason I'm here. They don't have much money to pay the bands but really wanted me to come and play for them so I arranged a couple of other gigs around it to help pay the costs. It sounds like it will be something out of the ordinary, and what with the Neverzillos and also Punk Lurex playing it will be quite a gathering of old friends.

But first, tonight's gig. By the time I start there are about sixty people on the terrace including quite a few teenagers who clearly came for the support band, but as soon as I start playing they pour into the club. It turns into a really good night, an enthusiastic audience comprising a good mix of ages. The kids stick around and a lot of them come to thank me for the show as I sit on the stage selling CDs afterwards. Then the Helsinki crew prepare to leave and Berja says he will pick me up from the hotel tomorrow at midday so we can all travel up to the farm together.

I should leave too, but the staff from the club invite me go for a drink with them in Bar Loose. We sit around sociably for a while, the people from the club insisting that anytime I want to come back and play I would be more than welcome. At around five in the morning I force myself to believe it really is time for bed, despite the fact it's still quite light outside, and I head back to the Omena, somewhat surprised that I'm there in about two minutes. Last February, in sub-zero temperatures and struggling with my luggage over the snow and ice in the darkness, covering the same distance seemed like an epic adventure.

11th June

Berja is waiting outside with the van at midday. We're going to drive to Tommi's place and then I'll wait there while he goes on to pick up the band's equipment. We have to take a lengthy detour around the waterfront to avoid the Helsinki Day celebrations in the town centre but it's interesting to drive through all these areas I've never had a chance to see before. Now I come to think of it, over the ten years I've been coming to Helsinki just about all I've seen of it has been the streets between the station and various clubs and hotels. We drive past the wealthy parts of town where luxury apartments have expensive views over the bay. People are strolling or sunbathing on the promenade, and on the sea hundreds upon hundreds of boats of all shapes and sizes are moored. 'Seems like everybody's dream is to own a boat,' says Berja.

But if owning a boat really was their dream, why – on this perfect sparkling Summer Saturday – aren't they out sailing on them?

Berja points out an old red brick building lying deserted. 'That used to be a waste water plant, but now the land here is too valuable for something like that. They will redevelop it but there are some toxins in there to dispose of first and they are not sure how to do that.' We drive on past the towering hulks of ferries destined for Sweden and Estonia. A little further on, as we reach the suburbs, Berja points out a large modern building on a hillside among some of the new apartments. 'That's the new waste water plant. They dug into the rock so they can do all the processing underground – they have to be very careful with emissions with all these people living around here.'

'Just curious, but what do you do as a job Berja?'

'I am in waste water management.'

Tommi invites me through to the small back garden where he and his wife Annastina are enjoying the sun. There are two budgies in birdcages, who soon get used to me and settle down to watch intently as I put a new set of strings on the guitar. Tommi says the best time of the year for the budgies will soon be here, when the flowers they like to eat most bloom, 'Those yellow ones, what are they called?'

'Buttercups?'

'Ah, yes – we call them butter flowers. *Build Me Up Buttercup*. I never knew what that song name meant before.'

Now he comes to mention it, I've no idea what it means now.

Berja arrives back with Janne and all the band gear, so it's time to leave for the festival, picking up the girl who sings for the band and her husband on the way. As the name suggests, the Neverzillos started off as a Rezillos covers band but only did the songs Faye Fife sang, and there weren't enough of those to fill a set. Now they have branched out to cover other classic songs from the punk era as well, and knowing Tommi's encyclopaedic knowledge of U.K. punk I can well believe it will be quite an eclectic selection.

We drive for a couple of hours until we reach the village of Kytollaika – 'don't blink or you'll miss it!' says Tommi – then on into the countryside until we see a hand-drawn cardboard sign for the gig with an arrow pointing down a narrow track towards a farmhouse a few hundred metres away. We pull up outside and are greeted by Satru, who lives here with his mum and organises the festival, now in its fourth year.

A home-made cart on two old bicycle wheels is pulled up to the van and we load the gear onto it, then roll it across the meadow to the backstage, a brick outbuilding containing the farm sauna. While the band unload I'm taken off to see the goats and their new kids before they get locked away when the music starts. There's always time to stroke a goat. Next to their field is the wooden barn where the bands will play. It's actually more the size of a shed; squeezing in more than fifty people would be ambitious. Overhead, long planks of wood are curing on beams just below the roof. There's a low wooden platform at one end of the dirt floor with a few bits of equipment on it, a small drum kit and some speaker cabs and amps, one of which ominously bears the name MONSTER MOSQUITO 60. At least sixty monster mosquitoes will probably be feasting on me later if I don't remember to put on the repellant.

Satru explains that he originally built the platform to keep the hay for the goats off the ground in the winter. When he finished it he stepped back and thought, 'That looks like a stage. Now I'm going to have to organise a gig here.' That's how the festival started. Now a mix of local farmers, villagers arriving on bicycles and punks driving in from all over Finland come. Satru tells me, 'We have to hold it at this time of year. Soon this place will be full of hay.' He reaches up and grabs a wooden pole hanging from the beams, which turns out to be a long-handled scythe. 'Better just remove this before the people arrive.' He walk off toward the farm looking like Old Father Time.

Berja is asked to move the van over to the official parking space – which is actually the road with a home-made 'P' sign staked in the ground next to it – because there's only room for one vehicle in front of the farm and soon one of the neighbouring farmers will come with 'a big bath tub on the back of a tractor.'

By now quite a few of the bands have arrived and there is a small gathering lazing around on the grass, most hugging the shadows to escape the fierce heat. Many are laying into the beers already, and one guys brings out a ten litre plastic container of cloudy home-brewed wine. 'Just like festivals in the old days!' sighs Berja.

The guy with the wine comes over to offer me a taste. 'We call it Challenge Juice,' he says. It's potent stuff. As I hand it back to him I notice a spot of blood dripping down my forearm. The first mosquito strike and I didn't even see it.

Satru brings out some bowls of excellent vegan food from the cold cellar below the sauna. The bands eat for free, the audience are asked for donations. 'Look at this,' he says, pointing at a sign pinned to the wall. 'That says, *maximum* donation ten euros. Nearly all the locals have put in twenty or more.' We both nod approvingly at their generosity, and then he says, 'Makes up for all the punks who will only pay one euro.'

The girl who told me about the big bath gives me a nudge. 'Here it comes,' she says. We wander up to the track where a tractor is just parking up, a trailer carrying a large round wooden barrel full of water attached to it. The girl tells me, 'We thought of having a sauna but we have this instead.'

'Because you're using the sauna as the backstage area?'

'Not just that. There isn't enough water in our well for all these people to use the sauna. If they did, we would have no drinking water for the next week.'

I go back to the hay shed, where the first of the bands is starting. The field that had the goats in is empty now, and on the closed doors of the barn next to it someone has pinned up a sign: *Shhh! The goats are sleeping!*

About twenty people have braved the furnace of the shed to watch the first band. Even inside in the shade there is no relief from the heat because the sun is beating down on the west wall and radiating through. Many people choose to watch through the doorway, myself included. Unlike most of the audience, I'm finding it hard to relax as I'm aware that there is still a long time before I am due to play. I'm scheduled to be the last act at around 10:30, still five bands to go including Punk Lurex, who – it suddenly occurs to me – still haven't turned up. The Neverzillos are due on after them, and as the second band get on stage I see Tommi through the door at the far side of the shed already in his stage gear in case Punk Lurex don't arrive in time and they have to go on next instead. His stage gear is a TV Smith 'Not A Bad Day' T-shirt and a kilt.

Punk Lurex turn up twenty minutes before they're due to start and we only have time for a hurried greeting. Tiina tells me that their regular guitarist couldn't make it so they've had to have a quick rehearsal with one of their former guitarists. She says that they just had time to run through their set and then try out Gary Gilmore's Eyes and Future Used To Be Better, in case I want them to join me on stage later. I ask her how they went in rehearsal and she says, '*Weeell…*'

I cry off. I haven't played the songs with Punk Lurex for years, and only Tiina and guitarist Kukka remain from that line-up. I've never even met the drummer or the (stand in) guitarist before and none of us have had a soundcheck. I think I have enough potential problems without adding to them.

One other thing bothering me is that there are no lights on the stage so no one's going to be able to see me by the time I play.

Then I remember: it won't get dark.

While Punk Lurex get their gear on stage I remember that I really ought to apply some mosquito repellant. I do have a bottle in my suitcase, but the thought of the stink of it and the idea of all those ghastly chemicals being absorbed into my skin, pores soon to be wide open as I sweat it out on stage, makes me reluctant to use it. Since that first bite on my arm I haven't really been troubled and I wonder if I might get away without it. Keen for some local knowledge, I ask Satru what he thinks.

He says, 'At the moment it's not too bad. If the wind comes up it may be okay.' His eyes drift across the field to the forest at the far edge of it. 'But they are in there, waiting.'

Hmm. And when they smell English sweat, no doubt they will gather together and say, *get him!*

Jukka, my friend and record label manager arrives with his wife Teija and a cooler box full of ice-cold beer. He offers me a bottle and I roll it soothingly over the swelling on my arm before drinking it. He also tells me that if I want I can come back and sleep at his place tonight and get a proper bed, rather than staying here on the farm as planned. This is good news. Sleeping conditions here seem a little uncertain. In fact, I haven't been shown anywhere to sleep yet but I had noticed two small tents pitched up by the farmhouse and I was getting a bit concerned.

Punk Lurex start their set, and the audience love them. I go to congratulate them afterwards and the guitarist mentions they could still play a few songs with me later if I want to risk it. I'm tempted, it's true, but still worried about the potential for things to go wrong. 'We could do it tomorrow at the Vastaviirta gig in Tampere,' suggests Tiina, and I agree that sounds a much better idea, hopefully we could even have a go at soundcheck to make sure everything will be okay.

The Neverzillos certainly take an unusual approach to the songs they cover. Not only do they translate all the lyrics into Finnish, but they make free with the arrangements too, often cutting out any extraneous instrumental passages, as well as changing some chords and vocal melodies. They're halfway through one song when I suddenly realise it's one of mine, 'The Servant,' which I recorded back in 1981 with The Explorers. As far as I know, no one's covered that before. By the time it's over I'm still not sure if it's been covered.

One more band to go. They seem quite popular and play a selection of Finnish hits, and the audience all sing loudly along. I'm the only one who doesn't know any of them. Then it's my turn. Most people have been outside getting some fresh air but when they see me getting on stage they start streaming back into the barn until it's packed. Unfortunately the lack of soundcheck soon shows. First there is no guitar audible at all, then it comes booming through the speakers at deafening volume. During the second song one side of the P.A. cuts out completely. Tiina's boyfriend Jukkeli rushes forward to help the sound guy change cables while I plough on, figuring that half the sound is better than none. The speaker continues to cut out intermittently over the next few minutes and the balance between vocal and guitar varies wildly, but then things settle down and with the worst of the problems out of the way I play for another two hours while people shout their appreciation, clap and laugh and kick up clouds of dust as they dance.

Exhausted and streaming with sweat, I sit on the stage and spread a selection of CDs out while people crowd round, keen to see what I have available. That's when I start to notice it: the mosquitoes have landed. They're moving around on my back, squadrons of them, just where I can't reach. There are rivulets of midges washing down my front in the sweat. They're on my eyelids. One guy sees me swatting ineffectually at myself, and comes up to the stage waving a little twig with a few leaves on it casually around his neck. 'This really helps,' he says.

I would need the whole fucking tree.

'Don't stay in one place or they will find you,' someone tells me, but that's easier said than done when you're negotiating the sale of CDs and books, and everyone wants to know which is the best one, and they only have a fifty euro note so you have to work out the change, and also they'd like to have your autograph on it, and most of all they want to let you know how much they enjoyed the gig and how much it means to them. It's important. Someone is telling me it's one of the best evenings she has had in her life and will never forget it. I can't really run off flapping my hands over my head and screaming, '*WAAAAH!*'

There's no sign of Punk Lurex as I pack my things away. Probably they are staking their place in a tent somewhere. I have never been so happy not to have to sleep in a tent. I say my goodbyes to everyone else and follow Jukka and Teija up the path towards the car. One of the girls who was dancing at the front insists on carrying my guitar for me and when we get to the road she says goodbye then jumps down the embankment and runs barefoot across the field back towards the farm. It's nearly two in the morning, twilight, and a heavy red moon hangs just over the horizon above the forests.

In half an hour we are in Tampere, indoors and insect free. Not only do I get a bed but a key to the entire adjoining self-contained apartment because Jukka's daughter is away. It's not dark yet so still time for one more beer.

12th June

A quick look at my back in the mirror confirms the expected damage. A tightly-packed patchwork of bites follows the contours of the vest I was wearing on stage last night. I count forty-seven just around the backs of my arms. Despite the vast number I'm surprised to find they don't itch as much as I'd expected, and mention it to Jukka over breakfast. 'No, they're not as bad as the mosquitoes in Lapland,' he says.

Click. Whirr. That's the sound of my brain filing away that snippet of information in case I ever I go to Lapland again.

We go for a walk around a nearby lake. People are in swimwear, some in the water, some sunbathing on the bank. From the opposite side of the lake we can hear the distant commentary as a rowing competition gets underway. Jukka tells me that in the winter they bore a hole in the middle of the lake and you can go ice swimming. (I bet they use a *kairata*.) I tell him, 'It's no good trying to convince me, I'm never going to do it.'

He admits he's only ever swum in an ice hole a few times himself. 'It's really not so cold,' he says. 'When you get out you can sit on the edge for a couple of minutes and you feel fine.'

I say, 'I'm *never* going to do it.'

We stop off at an art exhibition in a cabin up the hill and as we arrive a duo comprising two women, a singer and an accordion player, are just finishing a mournful tango to a crowd consisting of two people in deckchairs. At the end of the song the singer announces something, and the accordion player puts down her instrument. Jukka translates: 'They just said they are going to take a little break because they have been playing for four hours, but then they will come back and carry on.'

We walk back down the hill to the apartment. I point out one of the restaurants we pass, tables and chairs shaded by umbrellas on a high wooden sundeck projecting out over shrub-filled gardens. 'That looks a nice place. If I wasn't playing tonight I'd suggest dropping in for a beer.'

Jukka says it used to be a bar frequented by heavy drinkers. It's recently been refurbished and turned into a restaurant but has trouble shaking off its old clientele. He tells me that when it re-opened he went there with some friends for a meal. They had been at the table for a while enjoying the view down across the gardens when one of the bushes below them suddenly started shaking and a disheveled-looking man holding a six-pack climbed out from it.

Although most of my bites aren't too troublesome, there is one on my forearm that has swelled up considerably, and as I sit on the veranda at Jukka's place putting new strings on my guitar, I notice that my whole arm has begun tingling and I am having trouble gripping anything with my left hand. This doesn't bode well for playing guitar this evening. Jukka brings me some ointment that he thinks might reduce the swelling. While I'm rubbing it on, a mosquito bites me on the cheek. I know I'm delicious but it's daytime for God's sake.

I get a text from Tiina to say that Punk Lurex won't be able to play any songs with me tonight because guitarist Kukka doesn't get out of work until nine so won't be able to make it to soundcheck. I should turn up for my soundcheck around eight.

When I get to the venue I'm surprised to find it's a little upstairs room with a small low stage and tiny loudspeakers up on the wall behind it. I thought it was going to be the punk club with the large stage and PA system downstairs.

The advantage of playing upstairs is that it's free entry so there should be a good crowd in. Already there's a scattering of people who look like they have come for the gig, although many of them have clearly been here drinking for most of the day. There's no sign of Punk Lurex, just a few bits of drum kit at the back of the stage. The front of the stage is taken up by an old guy playing an electric organ, who stops playing when he sees me and asks if I want him to move his keyboard out of the way.

I say that would probably be a good idea as a whole band is going to be putting their gear on soon.

I'm wrong about the mosquito bites not being as itchy as English ones: over the last hour they have been driving me mad. Unable to stand it any more I go into the Gents to apply some anti-histamine cream. In the mirror I'm shocked to see the state of my back: the bites are red and have swollen grotesquely so that I look like I have plague boils. I decide to spare the audience this unpleasant sight, and remain in my sleeved T-shirt for the gig rather than change into the usual stage vest.

Punk Lurex still haven't arrived and neither has the sound guy so I get a beer and sit outside with Jukka. I explain about the bites and he says, 'Good job they are only mosquitoes. In some parts of Finland there are those other little animals – *punki*. They can be dangerous. You don't want to be a *punki* punk.'

When I don't laugh he says, 'Well, maybe that is not so funny when you translate it.'

Actually I'm too busy wondering what a *punki* is to think about the joke. After some detailed questioning I establish that it is the Finnish word for a tic. *Click. Whirr.*

Soon I see Tiina and Jukkeli parking in the street below and go down to greet them. I ask them why they don't have any instruments or equipment with them and Tiina tells me that Punk Lurex aren't actually playing tonight, they were only going to do that if we got the chance to play some songs together. I had been wondering why they weren't on the poster. Jukkeli, who booked the gig, mentions that I should start in ten minutes. Suddenly it's all happening. A confused-looking guy spots me as he walks up towards the club and asks me if I am TV Smith. I tell him I am. 'I am your sound engineer,' he says. 'I am sorry I am late. I have a bad toothache and am on strong painkillers so I am a bit high. But everything will be fine. I will just smoke this cigarette then I will go in and set up your microphone and you can start.'

I go indoors to tune up the guitar and a couple of minutes later the sound engineer comes up to the stage. 'I am your sound engineer,' he says. 'I am a bit high because I have a bad toothache and am on strong painkillers. Have I already said that?'

I tell him he has, and he apologises. 'I'm taking strong painkillers for this toothache,' he says. 'I will just go out for a cigarette and then you can start.'

He wobbles off to the door and I lean over to Jukkeli, who is setting up a merchandising stand, 'Please keep an eye on the sound, the engineer is off his face.'

It's getting on for ten when I finally start, though with the sun streaming in through the side windows it feels more like mid-afternoon. The sound is surprisingly excellent despite the doped-up technician, and in fact the only thing bothering me as I launch into the first song is that there is a powerful fan right behind me blasting me with air, cooling but very distracting. When the song finishes I explain to the audience that I'm going to switch it off because it's not a proper gig unless I work up a sweat. After fumbling around with the switches I succeed in stopping it and get a small cheer from the crowd. 'When all this punk rock falls through I could get a job switching off fans!' I tell them.

I play for two hours. Soon afterwards Jukka, who has to work tomorrow says goodbye and dashes home. I'll be staying at Tiina and Jukkeli's place tonight so I'm in no hurry. I chat to one of Tiina's friends who eyes up the swelling on my arm with some concern and says she has something that will help. She gets her bag and brings out a tin of some kind of ointment. 'This is really good,' she says. 'It's made out of tar and – I don't know what they're called, some herbs. It's organic.'

I rub some on. Now my arm smells of tar.

I speak to a guy sitting at the bar who used to drum for Punk Lurex. He mentions that he was brought up in Lapland so I ask him if it's true that the mosquitoes are much worse up there. 'Not really,' he says. 'It's just that there are more of them. Sometimes you see what you think is fog and it's actually just mosquitoes.'

Click. Whirr...

Eventually it's time to pack away. It seems too early somehow – it's still light outside, there's good music being played and there are still people hanging around drinking. I'm in a good mood, pleased that these three gigs have gone so well, and apart from being eaten alive by mosquitoes I've had a great time. Luckily the swelling on my arm didn't affect my guitar playing, and now I notice that the lump is going down a bit so even though I smell like a freshly waterproofed fence the mysterious ointment must be working.

The DJ has just put on *Obla Di Obla Da* by the Beatles, an unusual choice after an hour of reggae and garage tracks, but rather refreshing. I don't know what the remaining punks and elderly local alcoholics left in the bar make of it, but it comes as a pleasant surprise for me to realise that at last I'm over the grotesquely bland Marmalade version and can finally enjoy the song again in all its original McCartney-ness. I even find myself singing along:

Obla di obla da, life goes on – tar.

Finally, someone in the studio who knows what he's doing

Can I have my shed back please?

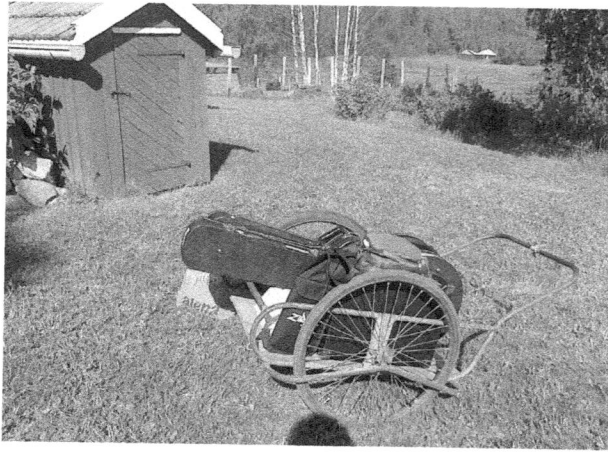

How to get the gear to
the stage

The stage

Me on the stage

12. FAR EAST (2011)

19th October

The land of the rising sun: I'd be able to catch a glimpse of it if only the stewardesses would let me open the window blinds, but that might wake the rest of the plane up.

I've never been able to sleep on planes myself, but this twelve hour flight would have been the perfect opportunity. Only 130 passengers, so as soon as the seat belt signs came off there was an inelegant dash to change seats and many people were soon stretched out across the middle rows in an economy version of the Business Class beds. Keen to look down at the passing world below, I switched to a window seat and was perfectly happy until just a couple of hours later, mid-afternoon UK time, when the stewardesses ordered the window blinds to come down and switched off the cabin lights to try and enforce a sleep regime for when we land in Japan at 9:30 in the morning, eight hours ahead of UK time.

An hour out of Tokyo the blinds come up and breakfast is served. Although I don't usually have a cooked breakfast, this time I relish the mini portion of fried potato and baked beans, for who knows when my next vegetarian meal will be. Friends who've visited Japan in the past have told me it's nearly impossible to find anything without meat or fish in the ingredients and the lack of any familiar language means risking anything that simply looks vegetarian would be a UMM or UFM minefield. If the worst comes to the worst, I have a stock of emergency vegan protein bars in my suitcase.

Once off the plane, there are a plethora of signs warning against unknowingly bringing any illnesses into the country, and masked doctors stand by the sides of sensors pointed at the disembarking passengers. A large board written in multiple languages states: 'Your body temperature is currently being monitored.'

The Japanese customs officials kindly prompt me to give the correct answers – 'What is the purpose of your visit? Sightseeing?' 'Yes.' 'And why do you have a guitar? Hobby?' 'Yes.' – so I get through mercifully fast and find myself spewed out into Tokyo airport earlier than expected only to find no one there to meet me. I sit in the garishly blue-lit free wi-fi 'Meeting Point' area and send promoter Tetsuya an email to say, just in case he's checking mails on the move, that I've landed and am waiting for him. I'm thirsty after the flight but don't have any change for the vending machine as all I could get from my local exchange bureau was the big stuff. (I held up the notes worth around £80 each in despair and said, 'Don't you have anything smaller?' and the guy behind the counter sort of sniggered and said, 'We don't get much call for Japanese Yen in Hammersmith.')

Anyway, the only water in the vending machine has the unappealing brand name *Pocari Sweat*, so instead I head across the terminal to buy a bottle from a kiosk. I'm embarrassed to have to hand over the large note, but the guy serving bows and smiles so much that I leave with the feeling that someone buying a 150 yen bottle of water with a ten thousand yen note was exactly what he had hoped would happen this morning. Soon after I get back to the waiting area I see Tetsuya heading across the terminal towards me.

I've met Tetsuya very briefly a couple of times in London, and have realised that although his grasp of English is better than that of many Japanese people – and considerably better than my Japanese, which amounts to one word: *sayonara* – it doesn't stretch to more than a few basics, so after the briefest of greetings he grabs my guitar and leads me outside to the airport bus for the ninety minute trip into Tokyo. Surprise: they drive on the left.

During the trip we try and talk about what will happen over the coming few days. I'll be playing two gigs at the weekend, half the set solo and half with a band from Tokyo backing me up on a few Adverts songs. I had expected to be going in to the rehearsal room with them today or tomorrow, but Tetsuya tells me there is only one practice planned, in two days time, the day before the first gig. That gives me nearly three days sightseeing: looks like I was almost telling the truth to the immigration official. The gigs are being advertised as 'The London Punk Sessions', and will also feature The Boys, who've been here three times before, and Menace, who like me are here for the first time. Both bands will arrive tomorrow.

'Then the question: what about food?' says Tetsuya. I've explained the situation to him by email many times over the previous months and now I do it again.

'No meat, no fish,' he repeats, then shakes his head and whistles through his teeth in a kind of embarrassed laugh. 'Tsss, tsss. tsss! So what *can* you eat?'

'I can eat noodles, rice, tofu,' I say, 'in fact, anything as long as there's no meat stock or fish stock in it...'

'Tsss, tsss, tsss!'

I'd thought that was the end of it, but he's clearly mulling over the problem, because after a five minute pause he suddenly turns back to me and says, 'We take you to supermarket!'

In the subsequent scraps of conversation as we enter the concrete maze of Tokyo's suburbs we do manage to establish that with unfortunate timing Tetsuya's helper in Vinyl Japan, the second-hand record shop he runs just around the corner from the hotel I'll be staying in, had an accident a couple of days ago and is currently in hospital, so Tetsuya is going to have to get back to the shop now and hand me over to his wife to look after me for the three hours before I can check in to the hotel.

'What happened to him?' I ask.

'Well, he smoking, fall out window.'

'Is he badly hurt?' I ask, shocked.

Tetsuya points at his backside. 'Broken,' he says. 'Maybe come back work tomorrow in wheelchair. Tsss, tsss!'

He also tells me that my hotel recently went bankrupt and now has a new owner – one of many establishments in Tokyo that have suffered a drastic loss of business since the earthquake and the Fukushima nuclear incident earlier this year, and which also almost certainly accounts for the empty flight. Tourism is significantly down. The bus takes us to Shinjuku station then we walk down the hill and over a busy road crossing towards the hotel. Already fatigued from the long flight, I'm overwhelmed with the noise and sights, people crushing in on every side, traffic, big screens blaring advertising films from the tall buildings around us, a subway train rattling across a bridge. Beside the bridge are a few narrow alleyways crammed with tiny ramshackle open-fronted restaurants. 'This place name Piss Alley,' says Tetsuya. 'Came idea for film Brade Lunner.'

Five minutes later we turn off into a side street and Tetsuya points out the hotel, and his wife Izumi who is heading down the road towards us. I leave my bags and guitar behind the reception desk, then Tetsuya goes back to the shop and Izumi asks what I'd like to do before I can check in. I tell her I can't even think straight after the flight, but perhaps we could discuss it over some coffee. Although it's just after midday here, for me it's just after two in the morning and my body is telling me it's time to sleep.

We order some coffee in a European-style place just around the corner, and I notice that they are advertising a 'veggie pizza' as one of their snacks. Handy to know it's here, just minutes away from the hotel. Slightly more alert after the coffee, I'm happy to agree to Izumi's suggestion of some sightseeing. I follow her through the bustling streets for a few minutes, then she hails a passing taxi and we climb in. I'd read in a guide book about the automatic doors on Japanese taxis but it still comes as a surprise when they flip open for you all by themselves. The taxi is spotlessly clean and the seats have embroidered white lace coverings. We get out a few minutes later at the entrance to Shinjuku park. Izumi buys a couple of entrance tickets from the machine, the barrier opens and we enter the park, an oasis of calm from the crowds and noise, skyscrapers towering over it on all sides. We wander along the winding paths to a temple built on the edge of a lake, where hundreds of giant koi carp writhe below, their gaping mouths thrust above water level in the hope of being fed by the tourists. Here and there groups of schoolchildren follow their teachers around the park, the pupils from each school wearing different coloured caps designed like helmets.

While we're walking back to the hotel I notice a fast food place called 'Freshness Burger' prominently advertising 'Vegetable Burgers' on the board outside and ask Izumi about it. She checks the board and tells me that there are two types: one with tofu, one with a bean burger, neither of them containing meat, and says that there's another branch of the chain near the hotel. Looks like being vegetarian here is not going to be as difficult as I'd feared. When we're nearly back, Izumi takes me to a supermarket where she buys me some water and fruit. One street further on, she points out a shop selling alcohol. 'Very cheap beer,' she says. 'Tell The Boys.'

She helps me check in then heads off back to the shop to help out Tetsuya, arranging for us to all meet again at 8:30 this evening to get something to eat. I take my suitcase and guitar up in the lift and find a very pleasant, if petite, room. There's hardly space to put down my luggage, but efficiently crammed in it is everything one could need and plenty one wouldn't: bed, fridge, desk, flatscreen TV, two small loudpeakers for iPod, internet cables, a torch that lights up when you take it off its wall clamp, trouser press, a wall fixing with coat hangers, shoe shine cloths and brushes hanging off it as well as a wire basket containing a spray bottle that could be shoe polish, or perhaps room deodorant or something entirely different. Probably best to leave it alone as all the writing on it is in Japanese characters, as it is on the gadget that at first looks like a paper shredder but could possible be a de-humidifier or air conditioner. Or heater. There's another gadget at the bottom of the wall that I suspect might be a vibration detector in case of earthquakes. The bathroom has a hi-tech electric toilet, with an arm at the side of the seat with a baffling array of buttons with no English explanation. One of the buttons has what is clearly a simplified diagram of water being sprayed up someone's bottom – I think I get the idea of what would happen if you press that – but the button next to it shows a diagram of a woman's head with flowing hair. Surely they're not expecting you to wash your hair in the toilet? It's a relief to find a conventional flush handle hidden away at the back of the seat.

So I'm installed in the room, and there are still a few hours to go before dinner. I've now been awake for 24 hours but want to resist falling asleep until tonight so I can stand a chance of adjusting to the new time zone. Consequently I use the time to try and solve a problem that's been concerning me recently. I've made a guest appearance on a single by Irish band Paranoid Visions and they have asked me to film a segment to include in their video, but as I've been on tour in Germany for the last three weeks I haven't had time to do it – and the deadline is next week. It occurs to me that with the little stereo set-up in the room, I could plug my laptop in and mime the track, filming it with my camera on video mode. My memory card would only have room for a few short clips but it would be better than nothing. I set up the track on the laptop and try placing the camera in a few positions, but the room is simply too small – the background is boring and to make it worse there's always some bit of hotel furniture in shot. The last thing you want in an anarcho-punk video is a trouser press. Pretty soon evening arrives and the room becomes too dark so I give up.

I head outside again and stroll around the area, always with an eye for potential vegetarian food. Most of the restaurants have plastic versions of the meals they offer in brightly-lit display cases outside. There are no English descriptions but it's clear that nearly everything is meat or fish.

I walk through Piss Alley, at this time of evening a smokey maze where Japanese businessmen and women are loosening their ties, sitting crammed together round counters, and having their chicken skewers cooked on charcoal grill boxes in front of them. Then I drop into a *pachinko* parlour where rows of people sit entranced before the garish fluorescent colours of their chosen machine and pump endless silver ball bearings into it from baskets at their sides, the continual crash of metal at thunderous volume wiping out the cares and stress of the day in a hypnotic sensory overload.

As fatigue weighs heavier and heavier on me I drag myself back to the hotel to meet Tetsuya and Izumi. We head to a nearby Indian restaurant where I have a very good vegetable curry and naan. I have now been awake thirty hours. Tetsuya arranges to come to the hotel at one tomorrow afternoon and take me out to see one of Tokyo's most famous temples, then I make my way back to the hotel and sleep.

20th October

I wake up at eleven, eat a banana, drink lots of water, take a shower and before I know it I'm feeling human. I go out for a coffee and another walk around the area, then meet Tetsuya back at the hotel. He tells me that he went out to the airport to fetch The Boys and Menace this morning. Right now they are in a nearby restaurant, and as soon as they can get into the hotel they will try to get to sleep so it looks like I won't see them today. Tetsuya is also re-thinking the idea of taking me to the temple this morning. 'Maybe tomorrow Boys and Menace like to come too,' he says.

'OK, so where shall we go?'

'Hmm, tall building, view of city?'

'Great!'

'Shrine?'

'Great!'

And off we go towards Shinkjuku station through the throngs of people.

As we make our way through the station and Tetsuya buys the tickets I keep a close watch on how it's done because I fully intend to try this solo at some point. We travel two stops along the overground Yamanote line and get out at Harajuku station. From there it's just a few steps to Shisuya-ku park, the entrance arched over by a huge wooden traditional *torii* gate. As we walk down the wide path through the woods towards the Meiji-jingu shrine, banks of brightly-coloured paper lanterns on either side, Tetsuya points out two young children in traditional costume and tells me that this month every year is a celebration for three, five and seven year olds so anyone who reaches any of those ages is likely to be dressed up by their parents. 'So that girl is probably three,' he says, pointing at the smallest, and I take a photo, unfortunately just as she falls over.

After a ten minute stroll, the path opens out to reveal another *torii* gate, with a large courtyard behind it ringed by traditional Japanese buildings. We wander up to the inner shrine, where entrance is blocked by a long offertory box covered with wooden slats. As we reach the barrier, a monk is approaching a large drum at the side of the sanctuary. Suddenly I feel Tetsuya grab my elbow. He presses a couple of coins into my hand. 'Throw in here,' he says, gesturing to the offertory box, 'clap twice and pray!'

I do as instructed, the sounds of the coin along with those from everyone else around me dropping through the bars with an atonal clatter. Then the monk starts to beat the drum, as large as a small car, with a long beater and plays a series of undulating rhythms that reverberate hypnotically around us, rising and falling in volume. I'm quite transfixed until Tetsuya nudges me again and gestures to the courtyard behind us. 'Traditional wedding starting. Very lucky! Take photo!'

The procession makes its way slowly across the courtyard, led by two monks in flowing white and purple kimonos, behind them the bride and female contingent of the family, closely followed by another monk holding a large pink Japanese umbrella over their heads. Then come the rest of the family and friends in smart modern costume. They all make their way along the side of the building and disappear somewhere into the inner sanctuary.

No sooner have I put my camera away than Tetsuya points out another kimono-clad girl, apparently in her late teens or early twenties. 'Photo!'

He hurries over and explains something to her and her parents, and before I know it I'm thrust next to her and having my photo taken – not only by Tetsuya but by the parents as well. The girl asks me in halting English where I'm from, and when I say London she looks thrilled. As we say goodbye, the parents initiate a lengthy series of bows which I do my best to reciprocate.

As we wander back up the path, Tetsuya mentions that in the event of a major earthquake he would be evacuated here to this park. We reach the gate, and he says, 'So now, back to the material world.'

With a vengeance. Across the road there is a network of clothes and novelty shops and food outlets clearly aimed at teenagers – 'Camden Market, Tokyo,' says Tetsuya – where gruff-voiced young men and women shout at passers-by to try and tempt them in. We hurry through, then hail a taxi to the Metropolitan Building. Once there, an elevator speeds us in seconds up to the 43rd floor where there is a stunning panorama of the city. 40 million people. Down there. Tetsuya points out the building that Godzilla climbed up.

We walk back to Shinjuku, then Tetsuya leaves me at the hotel so he can go back to work at the shop. I'm not really in the mood to hang around inside, so I head straight out again, determined to use the subway system before I forget how. Things don't start too promisingly when the ticket machine I choose turns out to be for long distance rail travel only, but a uniformed attendant spots my confusion and points me to the correct one. Then I'm through the gates and heading for the platform I used earlier. I noticed that this particular line does a large loop around the city via Tokyo's main station, which seems as good a place as any to head for – and if jet lag hits and I fall asleep at least I'll eventually end up back where I started.

It almost goes wrong straight away: a few minutes into the journey the train, packed with commuters, screeches to a halt, sending the passengers crashing into each other and resulting in a ripple of giggles and embarrassed apologies running along the length of the carriage. I only stay upright because I am so tired that I am hanging hard on to the overhead strap. An automated announcement explains, first in Japanese and then in English, 'The emergency brake has been applied.' I never find out why. After ten minutes we move off again.

Tokyo central station turns out to not be the best destination: it's in the heart of the business district, tall offices blocks all around. The Emperor's palace is in the area, but night has fallen and when I get to the entrance to the park where you can catch a glimpse of it, it's closed. I'm now extremely hungry, so as I wander around I drop into some of the malls and restaurant complexes scattered through the lower floors of the office buildings, becoming increasingly frustrated that there's nothing at all vegetarian on offer. I eventually find a few upmarket international restaurants in a mall below a bank, but even I'm not hungry enough to pay twenty quid for a small basic pizza.

So it's back to Shinjuku, where for the sake of variety I attempt the other Indian restaurant in the neighbourhood, a small room whose walls are crammed with Indian paraphernalia and framed photos of Ghandi. A few tables and chairs fill the cramped floor space, room for fourteen diners. I am the only one there. I order a pumpkin curry, and can hear the ingredients being chopped up in the kitchen behind the screen. When it arrives only a few minutes later it turns out to be very tasty. Finally with food in my stomach I feel myself reviving and go for a couple of hours walk around a part of the neighbourhood I haven't visited so far before finally heading back to the hotel and sleep.

21st October

The first person I see when I get down to Reception at midday is Honest John Plain from the Boys. 'How's it going John?' I ask cheerfully.

'Not so good Tim,' he replies, wincing and clutching his chest. 'Last week I fell off a wall and then went down a flight of steps. Broke two ribs.'

Also in Reception are a few members of Menace, as well as Jim The Vicar, a Boys fan who decided to use the concerts here as an excuse for a short holiday in Japan. It's also bass player Duncan's last gigs before he leaves the band so even more reason to come. I'm heading to the place round the corner to get some coffee and also to try the advertised 'Veggie Pizza,' and Jim says he could do with some coffee so he'll come with me.

On the way, I'm distracted by a crowd gathered in the small urban park next to the hotel. Something is clearly going on so I walk in to have a look and find a large white van with the words 'Earthquake Experience Vehicle' on the side. The other side of the van is open and has a small room with a couple of tables and chairs in it. As I watch, the Earthquake Experience starts up, and the two schoolgirls in the room scream with laughter and dive for cover under the tables as the van vibrates violently around them. 'You wouldn't want it to start up accidentally as they're driving back afterwards,' notes Jim.

Despite the language problems, the staff at the coffee place are only too happy to help me out with my order. Apart from all the usual varieties of coffee there's a choice of two types of veggie pizza. 'Would you like the one with ham or the one with chicken?' they enquire.

Breakfast can wait. Over coffee Jim, who actually *is* a vicar, tells me that he once used the lyrics to 'New Church' in one of his sermons.

Back at the hotel, I pop up to my room to devour one of my emergency vegan protein bars. Downstairs, most of the Boys and Menace and some of their wives and girlfriends have gathered for today's outing. With a party this size, Tetsuya and Izumi are both required to make sure no one gets lost. Presumably the guy with the broken bum is back at the shop. We are chaperoned through the teeming streets, Izumi leading and Testuya taking up the rearguard to make sure no one strays. We must seem a motley bunch to the suited Japanese office workers as we all pile on to the train.

Half an hour later we emerge at Asazuka station and in just a couple of minutes are at the entrance to Senso-ji, one of the biggest temples in Tokyo. To reach it you have walk along Nakamise Dore, a long parade of stalls selling a vast array of kitsch tourist items. The selection is so huge that the temptation to linger and investigate is great – but the price tag on even the smallest items is enough to make you move swiftly on. Anyway, we're here for a more lofty reason: the temple, a magnificent edifice surrounded by monastery buildings and a traditional five storey pagoda. At the entrance, visitors place sticks of burning incense – all decorated with the original, inverse swastika peace symbol – into wide bowls of sand and waft the smoke over themselves and into their hair for luck.

Our party agrees to meet up in an hour, then we each wander around on our own. I go up the steps to the temple, with its richly decorated walls and ceilings, the inner sanctum protected from the public by a glass wall. The only sound is the continual clatter of coins being thrown into the wide wooden offertory boxes and an occasional abrupt clap of hands from visitors as a precursor to prayer.

Outside I stroll through the formal monastery gardens, the path crossing a stream where giant koi swim. Further on, the gardens give way to a shabby street with a few tourist shops, and beyond a high wall I can glimpse the tops of thrill rides in a small, slightly run-down and curiously old-fashioned amusement park, distant screams of excitement as the drop ride releases.

Back at the temple steps the members of our party gather. Matt from the Boys arrives with Izumi, clutching an *omikuji*, a paper slip covered with Japanese script, purporting to tell his fortune. 'It's all bad,' he says.

Izumi hands the paper to Tetsuya and he reads through it grimacing and shaking his head. 'Tsss, tsss, tsss!'

To ward off the bad luck, Matt is instructed to go and tie the paper to the branch of a tree. That safely done, it's time to leave. We push our way through the crowds back to the entrance gate, then Tetsuya goes off with those of the group who want to eat, while the rest of us head back to Shinjuku with Izumi. Most of Menace are in our party. They want to eat too but first have to go to the Vinyl Japan shop to pick up the guitars they're borrowing for the gigs. I really want to eat but I'm not taking any chances: my destination is Freshness Burger.

The tofu burger turns out to be pricey and small, but tasty and reassuringly vegetarian. While I'm finishing it the guys from Menace walk past, checking out the menu in the window, and when they see me in there they come in, set down their guitar cases and order something too. The only other vegetarian in the entire crew, singer Finn, is also relieved to find something meat-free, though he tells me he did manage to get some vegetable tempura with no surprises when he went out for a meal yesterday.

While we're all chatting, I mention to drummer Noel about the video I'm supposed to be making with Paranoid Visions.

'Great lads, we've played with them in Dublin,' he says. 'How are you going to film it?'

'They want it on iPhone but I haven't got an iPhone. I've got a digital camera but I can't film more than a few clips on that.'

'I've got an iPhone. You can borrow that.'

'Really?'

Finn chips in: 'My girlfriend Robyn could film it. She loves all that. She's filmed stuff for the Red Hot Chili Peppers and loads of people. And she's got her HD camera here.'

Sounds like a plan.

Now it's time to finally start thinking about the gigs. Rehearsal is scheduled for 8:30 this evening, and Izumi arrives in the hotel reception on the dot of eight with a girlfriend who is so thrilled to meet me that she goes all giggly and has to keep covering her mouth with her hand.

Izumi soon spots Eddie, the guitarist who'll be in my band, waiting outside and I go to say hello. I like him straight away. We head down to the rehearsal room which is in the basement of the building just across the street – I can see it from the window of my room – and there Eddie introduces me to drummer Jossy and bass player Meg, 'Meg Advert,' he jokes. I'm quite surprised about this as when I checked the band out on You Tube they had a male bass player. Her eyes almost pop out of her head when she sees me and she gets so flustered that she trips over her guitar cable and falls straight into me. 'I love the Adverts!' she gushes. 'I love GAYE!'

And in fact she has clearly styled her look on Gaye. When we get into rehearsing, it turns out that she plays bass uncannily like her too, and I realise that calling the band the 'Tokyo Adverts,' as Tetsuya has advertised it, is going to be something close to the truth.

The band have learned the songs faithfully from the originals and we run through them a few times to iron out some small mistakes and get comfortable with playing together. Three hours later we're all done and looking forward to the gig tomorrow. We go upstairs to find Menace in an adjacent bar, and they wave me in to join them. 'I popped down to have a listen,' says Noel. 'It was sounding great!'

The members of the Tokyo Adverts are more or less non-drinkers and anyway need to get home and get some sleep ready for tomorrow, but I'm in the mood for a beer or two so I say my goodbyes to them and sit round a table in the Waterloo bar with Menace and their friends. The bar is a curious Anglo-Japanese hybrid, full of locals enthusiastically playing darts. I'm sat next to Robyn and we are soon discussing plans for the video. She says she's happy to film it and when I bring up the subject of location she suggests that we could possibly use the 'party room' on the top floor of the hotel. At least it would be worth checking it out to see what it's like. We make a tentative plan to try and find time tomorrow or the next day to do it, either there or maybe at one of the venues.

The time difference certainly does play tricks: before we know it, it's half past two in the morning, the bar has *run out of beer*, and Menace, who've been there since mid-evening, suddenly find themselves with a staggeringly high drinks bill, which takes some awkward pocket-searching to pay.

We could have carried on, but the potential switch from beer to *sake* was too potentially damaging to even consider. Apart from that one round.

22nd October

I wake up at eleven, fetch some coffee from Reception, then feast on one of the supermarket bananas for breakfast back in my room. I can feel a Freshness Burger will be required soon. Meantime I go up to the top floor of the hotel in the lift to check out the 'party room' for a potential location for the video. It turns out to be a large conference room with a picture window looking out onto the city skyline. Even better, I try a door next to it and find it opens onto a large outdoor balcony with an even better panorama and no glass in the way. This is the place.

Pleased with the discovery, I head out to Freshness Burger for breakfast and almost immediately bump into Finn and Robyn, both looking somewhat tired after last night's excesses. I tell them the news, and we agree to meet in a couple of hours. That will give us an hour to do some filming before the call to meet to go to the gig at three. Down the road in Freshness Burger, this time I order the bean burger version and lay into it like a starving man, which is pretty close to the truth. As I'm finishing, Boys bassist Duncan wanders past with his wife, checking the menu in the window, and when they see me in there they come in and order a veggie burger too. I should be sponsored by Freshness Burger. I chat with Duncan for a while about his plans for after he's left the band, then we wander back to the hotel, where the Boys have their call to go to the gig an hour before the rest of us and I have an appointment on the roof.

Robyn knocks on my door and comes in to have a listen to the song, then we take the lift up to the seventh floor. One disadvantage of filming outside is that there are no power points, so nowhere to plug in any external speakers. I have to mime the song while listening to it at extremely low volume through the tinny little speakers of my laptop, but the light and location are excellent and in half an hour we have finished, leaving ten minutes before we have to meet downstairs to go to the gig.

In my room I set up an internet Dropbox site so I'll be able to send the files to the band, then when head down to Reception. I thank Robyn again for helping out and tell her Paranoid Visions will be really pleased that we managed to do it. 'It was a pleasure,' she says. 'And by the way, thank you for curing my hangover.'

We all follow Izumi to Shinjuku station, where we take a ten minute train journey to Shimokitazawa and emerge into a lively shopping street. Five minutes walk down it we arrive at tonight's venue, the 251. It's a standard rock venue, down in the basement, with room for about 200 people, a small dressing room at the back of the room by the bar. The Boys have just finished their soundcheck and Menace immediately start setting their gear up on the stage – it's a while since they last played so they are keen to get some rehearsal in. My soundcheck is scheduled in an hour, so I head up on to the street for a look around and hopefully to find some food. I'm in luck: just up the road there's a caravan set up in a yard selling what appears to be a vegetarian pizza, and the woman running it knows enough English to confirm it contains no meat. It's only small and costs the equivalent of about seven pounds but my body is crying out for food. I place the order, pay, then go to sit at an outdoors bench. While I'm waiting I suddenly start to notice that I feel unbearably tired. I start to shake and feel queasy and become convinced that I'm going down with some dire illness or food poisoning and won't be able to play.

Luckily as soon as I have some food inside me I begin to feel better, and realise that without noticing it I'd drifted into a jet lag slump. Concerned that I'll be needed at the venue by now, I hurry back down the road and arrive just as Menace are leaving the stage. I have a lightning fast soundcheck for my solo set, then my band get on stage with me and set their equipment up. When they're all ready I ask Eddie which song he'd like to run through for soundcheck. 'All of them,' he replies.

So we do, and they sound even better than last night.

Gigs in Japan start considerably earlier than in Europe, so the normal wait to play is a lot shorter than usual tonight. Doors open in an hour at six, then I'm scheduled to start an hour after that. In the dressing room, Meg surprises me by showing me the T-shirt she's intending to wear for the gig tonight: it's a hand-made replica of Gaye's notorious 'Fuck Off' T-shirt from 1977. She really has been studying the role.

Out in the club, people have already started coming in despite the early hour and I bump into my friend Ako, who used to run a stall in Camden Market as the 'Blabla Nurse' making wristbands that she called 'bandages' that I have taken to wearing on stage ever since. She moved back to Tokyo to carry on her fashion business there and I haven't seen her since. She has a present for me of some new wristbands and a pack of green tea for Gaye. A few other people recognise me and ask me to sign records. By seven, the place is nearly full. Things are looking promising.

I know I have my work cut out to play a solo set to a roomful of people who won't have heard the songs before or understand any of the lyrics, so I hit the stage running, almost literally, and power through a half hour of songs with barely any pauses. I get polite but enthusiastic applause after the songs, which ramps up a bit when I introduce the occasional Adverts song among the solo material, and people stay watching and listening for the whole thing so I'm pretty pleased with how it went. Then I put my guitar down and introduce the band, and for almost fifteen minutes, five songs, it's like being transported back to 1977 – the audience going nuts, the band behind me playing the old Adverts songs in an uncannily authentic copy of the originals.

Back in the dressing room, the band are overwhelmed with how much they enjoyed the gig and I'm really happy with their performance too. Before I left the UK I'd had some misgivings about whether or not it was a good idea to get involved with another pick up band or if it would just be better to play the gigs here solo, but now seeing the look of joy on their – and the audience's – faces I know it's been worth doing.

I watch Menace from behind a barrier down the side of the club, then while the Boys play I go out into the audience and have a drink with Ako, and get my photo taken with a lot of the local punks who all want to tell me as best they can how much they love the Adverts and how much they enjoyed tonight.

The plan now is to get back to the hotel and – for the English musicians at least – wind down with a few beers in the Waterloo bar; a plan thwarted when we pile out of the taxis to find it closed for the weekend. Instead we head down the road to a restaurant the others have been in before, and which they say has a few veggie dishes.

The restaurant has one long wooden table running down the centre of the room, a selection of around thirty individually priced tempura dishes in baskets on a counter on one side. Izumi carefully points out to me the three or four that don't contain meat or fish: one with pumpkin, one with lotus, and one with a chopped carrot and onion mix. Cold vegetables in batter is not my idea of the perfect meal but I'm hungry, and hey, it's the first authentic Japanese food I've had since I arrived. Even better, there's a beer-pouring machine. You locate your beer glass in it and put a coin in the slot: the beer begins to pour and simultaneously the platform holding the glass glides out to the perfect angle to stop the beer frothing up. Just as the beer reaches the top of the glass, the cradle glides back to the upright position and the tap dispenses a final spurt of beer to provide the perfect head. I can see many of our party wondering if it would be possible to fit one of those things in their suitcase.

23rd October

I had been hoping for a lie-in, but annoyingly wake up at 7:30 and immediately realise sleep is over for the day. I decide to use the extra few hours for some souvenir shopping. Unfortunately even the tackiest souvenir shops have eye-wateringly high prices and the kind of gimmicky item that might seem funny if it costs a couple of quid loses its appeal when it costs ten times that. There are a few food shops, normally ideal for gifts for the folks back home, and If I wanted to lash out a small fortune on a snack bag of dried baby crabs, this would be the place to come. I soon give up on shopping and decide to look for something to eat, but even here in Shinjuku on one of Tokyo's main shopping streets there's precious little vegetarian fare. Eventually I come across a branch of Freshness Burger so I go in and have the usual.

I'm back at the hotel in time to put a new set of strings on the guitar before all the bands meet in Reception. Led once again by Izumi, we head up the road to take the metro to Shindaita station. The club 'Fever' is situated right opposite the exit, and I see Meg waving at us from over there. 'Are Eddie and Jossy here yet?' I ask her.

'Eddie not here...' she tells me, then runs out of English words and resorts to gestures. Communication is a constant problem – I haven't had a chat with a Japanese person that lasted more than a few hesitant sentences since I got here.

The club is a similar size to yesterday. Once again the Boys have just finished their soundcheck and some of them are hanging out in the spacious dressing room backstage along with a couple of local bands. While Menace set up their gear I go outside to enjoy the warm late Autumn sunshine and take a stroll. As I head up the street I hear a voice shouting my name, and see Duncan beckoning me from the door of a restaurant so go and investigate. Duncan and Honest John are both sat at a window table with a meal in front of them. 'John is certain that this,' – he gestures at the bowl in front of John – 'has no meat or fish in it.'

I check out the noodles in broth as John turns it over with his chopsticks. 'No meat in there,' he says.

'But that looks like meat stock,' I say.

He tastes a bit. 'You could be right...'

On up the road, but the shops peter out, and I notice Jossy heading in my direction clearly on a mission to bring me back to the club. Meg is already on stage but there's still no sign of Eddie. Tetsuya appears next to me and tells me, 'Eddie in traffic.'

'Do we know when he'll get here?' I ask. 'Will he make it in time for soundcheck?'

'Ah… Tsss! Tsss! Tsss! Sorry!'

So I get on with my acoustic soundcheck, then keep the guitar on and play through a couple of songs with Meg and Jossy. That will have to do, even though it's completely different from how it will sound with electric guitar.

'Are you sure he's actually coming,' mentions Duncan as I get off stage. 'You know how the Japanese can't say no – if he wasn't able to come, would they tell you?'

Cheers, Duncan, for setting my mind at rest.

Backstage I do an interview for a Japanese punk fanzine, translated by a German guy living in Tokyo, who knows PamP and thinks it would be a great idea for Garden Gang to play over here.

By the time I finish the interview I'm very hungry. There is a vegetarian pizza on the club menu, but it's only a couple of hours until I play so I can't risk it. Instead I eat the last emergency vegan protein bar. Tomorrow I'll be heading home, so no need to save it any longer.

I have a chat with Meg about the gig and notice she's looking a bit sad. 'You're leaving tomorrow,' she says, and mimes tears running down her face. 'I'm crying,' she says, and then she does, and then she has to go and put her make-up on again.

Honest John walks by. 'You've still got it Tim,' he mutters.

Eddie rushes in and apologises for not being able to get here for soundcheck. 'I have a present for you,' he says, and hands me over a plastic bag with two cans of beer in it. 'These best beer in Japan!'

What a guy! Exactly what I need right now as I get into gig mode.

People are a bit slower to come in than last night and I can see Tetsuya looking anxious – he clearly has a lot riding on these gigs after the cost of getting me and two bands over here as well as all the other expenses. All the same, there are already about forty in when the first band go on at six. They're a Japanese version of a mod band called The Chords, with the original English lead singer who's living over here. 'Going on to no one,' he says as he heads for the stage. 'Typical Chords situation.'

I go and watch from out front and the band are pretty good, but the audience is reserved, hanging back from the stage, the smattering of applause quickly dying out after each song.

After that it's a band led by the Japanese guy with the punk fanzine, but I don't watch them because it's getting too close to my own show. My second one in Japan and the last one of the trip so I intend to make it count.

I plug in and get straight into it, putting a few different songs into the set from yesterday and including a few more Adverts ones so people have something familiar to grasp onto. The club is nearly full by now and there are a few familiar faces in the audience from last night. I get the distinct impression that already people are getting used to the idea of a punk solo set, and that it's going down well – there's even some muted singing along – but it's hard to get used to the way the applause at the end of the songs disappears almost as soon as it's begun. I don't let it get me down, smashing in to the next song with only the minimum gap. Forty minutes later the band come on and we dash through the Adverts songs to a similar reaction to yesterday, slam dancing and air punching in the crowds. I lean over the barrier and the first few rows all sing along with the hits.

Then a strange feeling: all this way for these two gigs and now I'm all done.

I go and mingle with the audience, soak up their reaction, get my photo taken a few times and sign a few records. I meet a guy from Boston who tells me that the last time he saw me I was being backed up by the Midnight Creeps, from nearby Providence. Then I get chatting to a guy from Japan who's friends with Jonathan from Suzy & Los Quattro.

When the audience leaves there's a half-hearted attempt at an after-show party – only partially successful because we have to buy our own drinks, and there's no food because the kitchen is closed – then we gather on the street while Tetsuya and Izumi hail taxis to take us back to Shinjuku. I end up in Eddie's car along with Meg, who looks sadder than ever that it's all over. We all agree that if I ever get an invite back to Japan we'll do this all over again, and they'll learn a few more songs so we can do a longer set together.

Back in Shinjuku, some cold tempura and a beer machine are waiting.

24th October

When I get down to Reception at seven in the morning Tetsuya and Izumi are already there and seem surprised that I'm so punctual, packed and ready to go. Not as surprised as I am when one minute later Eddie walks in. He looks tired but he's made the trip especially to say goodbye again, and to hand over a couple of small gifts for me and Gaye.

Tetsuya grabs the guitar and walks me up to the airport bus stop outside Shinjuku station. Monday morning, and all the suited office workers are back on the streets, hurrying to their jobs. As I walk up past Piss Alley I realise that everything that seemed so alien to me just a few days ago now has an air of familiarity. These streets are now my neighbourhood. People who I'd never even met when I arrived are now my friends. I'm genuinely sad to be leaving.

Tetsuya and Izumi wave at me from the other side of the window as I take my seat, and the bus moves off into the morning traffic and out through the suburbs of Tokyo towards the airport.

Regulation tourist photo (1)

Regulation tourist photo (2)

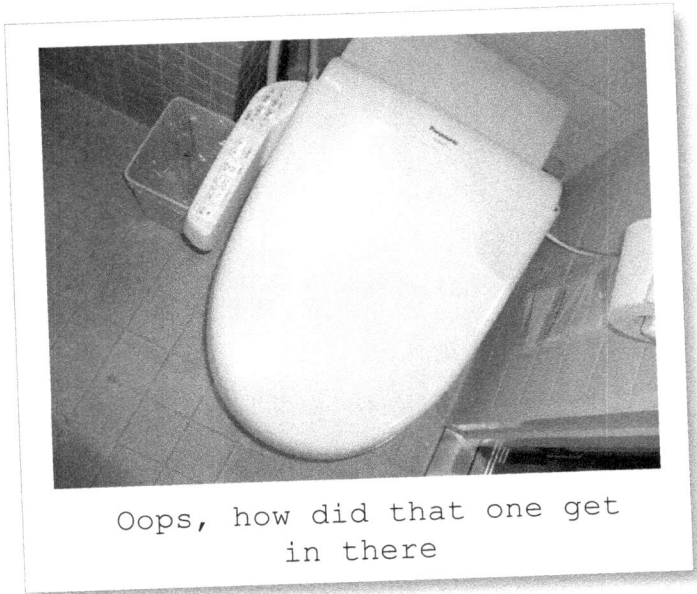

Oops, how did that one get in there

Completely vegetarian. But plastic

Lucky

Exploiting the locals

Earthquake machine

In bandages with the
blabla nurse

The Tokyo Adverts

www.ingramcontent.com/pod-product-compliance
Lightning Source LLC
Chambersburg PA
CBHW080515090426
42734CB00015B/3066